D1207011

Books by Louise Bush-Brown

FLOWERS FOR EVERY GARDEN
YOUNG AMERICA'S GARDEN BOOK
MEN WITH GREEN PENS

with James Bush-Brown
PORTRAITS OF PHILADELPHIA GARDENS
AMERICA'S GARDEN BOOK

GARDEN BLOCKS
FOR URBAN AMERICA

NEIGHBORHOOD GARDEN ASSO'. MEMBER

GARDEN

BLOCKS

FOR URBAN AMERICA

Louise Bush-Brown

712.6
B
c.1

CHARLES SCRIBNER'S SONS ❖ New York

MADISON COUNTY LIBRARY
CANTON, MISS. 39046

Copyright © 1969 Louise Bush-Brown

This book published simultaneously in
the United States of America and in Canada—
Copyright under the Berne Convention

All rights reserved. No part of this book
may be reproduced in any form without
the permission of Charles Scribner's Sons.

A—3.69 [RZ]

Printed in the United States of America
Library of Congress Catalog Card Number 69-17051

Dedicated to MRS. LYNDON B. JOHNSON

in recognition of her devotion to the ideal

of a more beautiful America and for

her inspiring leadership and accomplishments.

An old man plants his flowers with loving care

"All the flowers of all the tomorrows are in the seeds of today."
—*Chinese Proverb*

GARDEN BLOCKS FOR AMERICA'S CITIES

On a bleak February day in the winter of 1953 a group of citizens met in Philadelphia to discuss the possibilities of stimulating a sense of neighborhood pride in the blighted areas of the city.

In the group were the Directors of several Settlement Houses and Community Centers, the Administrative Head and the Home Advisor of one of the large Public Housing Projects, the Principal of a large elementary school, and a number of other concerned citizens.

We were all well aware of the conditions in the vast, underprivileged areas within the city, and the idea was presented to the members of the group that perhaps much could be accomplished in encouraging neighbors to work together to improve their communities through the organization of constructive garden projects.

Someone recalled the ideal in the mind of William Penn when he gave the following instructions to the three Commissioners whom he sent to lay out the city of Philadelphia on the banks of the Delaware River in the year 1682.

"Let every house be placed, if the person pleases, in ye middle of its platt as to the breadth way of it, so that there may be ground on each side for Gardens and Orchards, or fields, yt may be a Greene Country Towne, which will never be burnt and will always be wholesome."

The ideal of William Penn was so heartily accepted by the early colonists that they were able to maintain their city as a Greene Country Towne for more than a century and a half. Surrounding almost every home there were trees and grass and gardens. But with the coming of the industrial era Philadelphia gradually lost the aspect of a Greene Country Towne. With pressures of growth and concessions to expediency the people began to lose sight of Penn's ideal and gradually, over the years, the city became more and more congested, and over-crowding brought misery to thousands of citizens. The result for many was the loss of initiative and the apathetic acceptance of their surroundings.

"And to-day," someone in the group remarked, "you can walk for miles in this city without seeing a tree or a flower, or even a vestige of green or growing things."

After a pause someone spoke of the cities and towns in Europe where the flowers contribute almost as much to the charm of the community as does the picturesque architecture. And so often in Europe material poverty is clothed with flowering beauty, showing that there is no poverty of the spirit.

We mentioned the cottage gardens of England, the roses in the cottage gardens in Scotland, the gardens at the railway stations in Sweden and Italy and England, the little gardens on the high station platforms in Holland, cared for by the signal men, and the terraced plantings on the railway bunkers at Ostende. One member of the group told how impressed she had been with the flower boxes in the beautiful Swiss city of Bern where almost every window had its flower box. And she mentioned that it was in Bern that the idea came to her that perhaps in Philadelphia we might be able to do with flowers what nothing else could do.

As a group we voiced a deep regret that so many American towns and cities had failed to recognize how much flowers could add to the charm and beauty of a community.

When people from Europe visit America they are almost invariably impressed with the drabness of so many of our small towns and villages, and are shocked by the tragic neglect of the blighted slum areas within our large cities.

It was the consensus of feeling on the part of those attending the meeting that if a few constructive garden projects could be initiated they might prove to be a catalyst which would stimulate an upsurge of community pride.

The suggestion was made that each of the Settlement Houses represented at the meeting organize a Garden Group, and that flower boxes be planted on a few pilot blocks. Several of the Settlement Directors were enthusiastic, but a few were highly skeptical. The leader of the group was told that she was entirely too visionary. "You don't know these areas," said the head of one of the Settlements. "You talk about window boxes. They wouldn't stay there 24 hours! The flowers would be snatched out and the boxes destroyed. You wouldn't be able to cope with the vandalism and you would find nothing but apathy on the part of the people on the blocks. Such a project would be doomed to failure."

The leader of the group replied. "I would rather try it and fail than not try it at all."

In the discussion that followed the suggestion was made that a few garden projects be organized for both adult and youth groups at several of the Settlements and one of the Settlements agreed to start a pilot Garden Block.

It was felt that such a program could best be accomplished through an organization dedicated to this purpose and all present were in agreement. Several names for such an organization were suggested. The final vote was in favor of The Neighborhood Garden Association of Philadelphia.

It was proposed that the motto of the Association be the admonition which Edward Bok's mother gave her son when, as a young man, he migrated to America.

"Strive to make the world a little better and more beautiful
because you have lived in it."

A Chairman was appointed and a representative of each group present agreed to serve on the Committee.

As the meeting drew to a close the Chairman quoted the ancient Chinese proverb

"It is better to light a candle
Than to curse the darkness."

and she added

"Perhaps we have lighted a candle
here this afternoon which, in the years
to come, will shine unto many."

A week later the Chairman invited the Presidents of the suburban Garden Clubs to attend a meeting in Philadelphia to discuss the possibility of participating in this new program. Almost every Garden Club was represented at the meeting.

The special problems of the city gardener were considered,—the lack of knowledge and experience, the difficulties of growing sturdy plants under city conditions, the hazards of vandalism, but it was agreed that with intelligent and understanding guidance many of these limitations and handicaps could be overcome.

The Chairman mentioned that she was preparing a small booklet which would give simple, explicit directions for the care of plants which she thought would be very helpful for these beginning gardeners. We all realized that in the early stages this would be essentially a teaching program.

The Presidents of the various Garden Clubs were asked to present to their members the opportunities for service which the program offered. The response was enthusiastic and most heartening for The Neighborhood Garden Association Committee. Eighteen Clubs agreed to become a sponsor of one of the projects.

Sponsorship involved taking an active interest in one of the programs developed at a Settlement House or at the Public Housing Project, and providing the plants needed for the project. Members of the Garden Clubs were asked to "Grow to Share"—to make cuttings of house plants, to plant a few extra seeds, to divide perennials and bulbs or, if anyone preferred, plants could be purchased at wholesale rates.

The next step was the organization of the pilot garden groups at the Settlement houses. Attractive posters were made to be put in the windows at each of the Settlement Houses and a sample window box was made and filled with flowers and put on view where all could see it, and it was not long before a number of groups had been formed.

At the next meeting of the Neighborhood Garden Association Committee several important decisions were made. It was agreed unanimously that all the programs must be at the grass-root level with as much of the initiative as possible coming from the residents in the area.

It was further agreed that each Garden Block would be sponsored for two years. It would then become an Independent Block and would be responsible for obtaining its own flowers. However, the plants could be ordered at wholesale rates through the Neighborhood Garden Association. The block would continue to be a member of the Association and would be eligible for all privileges and awards. The following guidelines were set up for Garden Blocks.

1. Application to become a Garden Block should be made by a resident on the block or by a committee from the block.

2. At least 80% of the families on the block should agree to participate in the program. Thus it would become a community program, neighbors working together.

3. On each block there must be a Garden Block Leader, either a man or a woman, who would take responsibilities and would work closely with the Settlement House and the Neighborhood Garden Association.

4. The boxes should be made by the men and boys on the block, according to the specifications provided by the Association, or boxes having the approval of the Association could be purchased if desired.

5. The boxes must be prepared for planting according to the instructions in the booklet supplied by the Association.

6. High standards should be maintained in keeping the block clean.

The Chairman presented the members with a copy of the booklet which she had prepared for new Garden Blocks, reproduced below:

GARDENING TOGETHER

YOUR GARDEN BLOCK

"Strive to leave the world a little better and more beautiful because you have lived in it."

As a resident on a new Garden Block we are happy to welcome you as a member of the Neighborhood Garden Association of Philadelphia.

This spring you and your neighbors will have flower boxes at your windows. Perhaps a climbing rose can be planted in a little bay beside your doorstep. If there is a vacant lot on your street perhaps, with everyone co-operating, it can be made into a tot-lot or a lovely little garden.

One of the greatest joys of gardening is the happiness which comes from the sharing of one's flowers with others. And a window box offers very special opportunities for this sharing of beauty, for to friends and neighbors and to all who pass along the street it gives a lift to the heart just to look at it.

We hope that you will help your block to become an Award Winning block this year. To qualify for an Award-of-Merit every flower box or container on the block must have good care and high standards must be maintained in keeping the block clean.

What you and your neighbors do on your block to make it beautiful will be a source of inspiration to people on other blocks in your vicinity, and perhaps even to people in other cities, for Philadelphia was the first city to have Garden Blocks, and visitors from other parts of the country who see them take the idea back to their own communities.

The Lord meant our world to be beautiful. When one goes out into the country one sees grass and trees and flowers everywhere,—the natural beauty of the countryside which God has created for all to enjoy. And when you make a little garden at your window, or when you take a little plot of ground in the city which would otherwise be bare and ugly and make it beautiful with flowers, you are working in harmony with God, for you are helping to make the world a more beautiful place in which to live.

MAKING YOUR WINDOW BOX

In order to obtain the greatest satisfaction from your window box it is necessary to have a box which will provide favorable conditions for growth of your plants.

WOODEN BOXES. A window box made of good, sound wood will last for many years. There is a great difference between a well-built flower box and one which is carelessly knocked together. When making a box the following points should be considered.

1. Use a good grade of lumber. Some woods are particularly resistant to decay. Cedar, cypress and white pine are excellent.

2. Wood not less than ¾ of an inch in thickness is best, although for small boxes lighter wood may be used satisfactorily.

3. A good width for the average box is 8 inches (inside measurement) and the depth should be about 8 inches. The length will depend upon the location in which the box is to be placed.

4. In constructing a box screws are better than nails as they will not pull out so easily.

5. As there is considerable pressure against the sides of a flower box, it is advisable to use angle irons or a piece of steel tape on the inside of the box at the corners in order to reinforce it.

6. Adequate provision should be made for drainage by boring holes in the bottom of the box ½ inch in diameter, spaced 6 to 8 inches apart.

7. Do not make a saw tooth edge on the front of your box as the water will run off through the notches.

8. The box should be level when it is put up. This is important. If the box slopes the water will run off and will not reach the roots.

9. White paint makes a box look attractive as it shows the plants off to good advantage. Mouldings around the edge add to the appearance of a box.

METAL BOXES. Window boxes made of very thin metal are not recommended. Metal is a conductor of heat and in hot summer weather the soil becomes so over-heated that the plants cannot thrive, if they are on the sunny side of the street. Also, tin boxes are often so shallow that they do not provide good growing conditions and they soon rust out. A good wooden box will outlast a cheap tin box by many years.

PREPARATION AND PLANTING

DRAINAGE. It is important for window boxes and any other type of container in which plants are grown to have good drainage. If this is not provided, surplus water cannot drain off during periods of heavy rain, the soil will become soggy and the plants will suffer. On the bottom of your box put an inch layer of old bricks smashed into small pieces, or coarse gravel or small stones.

SOIL. Good top-soil should be obtained if possible. If the soil is a heavy clay which gets muddy when wet and becomes hard on the surface when dry, get a small bag of Michigan peat and mix it thoroughly with the soil. Peat moss may be used, but it is important that you wet it until it is moist and crumbly before you mix it with the soil. Fill your box with soil up to within one inch of the top. If it is too full the water will run off and not get to the roots.

PLANTING TIME. At the time of planting the soil in your box should be moist but not too wet. It is better to have it a little too dry than too wet and muddy. If it rains the day or night before planting, place a heavy layer of newspaper over the box to keep it from getting too wet.

Plants must be handled with care at time of planting. Do not let the roots be exposed to the sun for even a few minutes. Plant immediately after you have taken the plant out of the container. Set it so it is level with the soil in the box and press the soil firmly around it. The best way to remove a plant from a flower pot is to place the first two fingers of the left hand over the earth in the pot; then turn the pot upside down and knock the rim of the pot against a wooden surface. The plant should drop out easily and the roots will not be disturbed.

As soon as all the flowers have been planted, water the box thoroughly. If the plants show signs of wilting, shade them with a loose sheet of news-paper or cardboard.

THE CARE OF YOUR FLOWERS

In order to make vigorous growth and give good bloom over a long period your plants need five essential things; food, water, air, light and good care.

FEEDING. Unless you have very rich top-soil in your box it is wise to feed your plants every 2 weeks. Buy a small package of plant food such as Grow-Stuff or Rapid-Grow. Dissolve 1 level teaspoonful in 2 quarts of water and pour a cupful about each plant. The soil should be moderately moist when the application is made.

WATERING. Be faithful about watering your flowers. How often your box should be watered will depend upon whether it is on the sunny side or the shady side of the street; whether it is sunny and hot, or cloudy; whether your soil is light and sandy and dries out quickly or of a heavy type which dries out more slowly. Under average conditions a thorough watering once a day is usually sufficient. A light watering does little good as it wets only the upper few inches of soil and does not get down to the roots. In very hot weather two waterings a day may be necessary if you are on the sunny side. In cloudy weather water less frequently. Do not over-water. The soil should be kept moist but should never be soggy. Never let water get on the blooms when the sun is on them, as it will burn and spot the petals.

One thing that is important to understand and to remember is that the only way in which plants can make use of the nutrients in the soil is to absorb them through the tiny hairs on their roots after the nutrients have been dissolved in water. Therefore if you deprive your plants of water you are not only causing injury to the cell structure of the plant, but you are also starving your plants, as they are unable to obtain any food from the soil.

In the soil which has become completely saturated with water the air which is normally present in the soil is driven out, being replaced with water. If this condition continues for any length of time, the plants begin to turn yellow, and become sickly and die because they are being deprived of the oxygen which the air in the soil normally provides. This condition is more apt to happen in heavy clay soils than in light, sandy soil.

LIGHT. Plants vary greatly in the amount of light which they require. Most plants which flower abundantly,—such as petunias, geraniums, lantanas, marigolds, verbenas and zinnias, require a great deal of sunlight in order to bloom well. Many foliage plants and a few flowering plants such as begonias and fuchsias require partial shade. Coleus and impatiens will do well in either full sun or partial shade. Very few plants can be grown in deep shade or under an awning where they receive no direct light at all.

GOOD CARE. One of the most important points is to nip off all the faded flowers in order to prevent them from setting seed. If you do this promptly and faithfully your plants will continue to bloom for many months. On petunias be sure and nip the faded flower off just below the little green cup at the base of the petals. When you remove a faded geranium bloom slide your finger down to the base of the stem and snap it off with great care so as not to harm the rest of the plant.

If you are ill and cannot look after your flowers, or if you are going to be away, be sure and ask a friend to look after them for you. She will be glad to do it, for that is part of being a good neighbor.

SETTLEMENT HOUSE PROJECTS

SAINT MARTHA'S SETTLEMENT

The first Garden Block in America was planted on the 700 block of Mercy Street in South Philadelphia on the 7th of May, 1953.

The window boxes had been made in the workshop at the Settlement

Planting the first Garden Block in America

The same block two years later

Before

A Garden Block

After

A summer afternoon

Planting day

Before

A Garden Block

After

and were up and ready for planting on that lovely May morning, and the people on the block were eagerly awaiting the arrival of the members of the sponsoring Garden Club Committee. At last the station wagons loaded with plants turned into the street. The Block Leader, the Director of the Settlement and the Chairman of the Neighborhood Garden Association were there to welcome the members of the committee from The Gardeners which was the sponsoring club.

The plants were unloaded—gay geraniums, colorful petunias, lantanas and vinca vines, and the residents gathered to observe the planting of the first window box. It was a gay and happy sight to watch the members of the Garden Club Committee going up and down the block, chatting with the people and helping wherever help was needed.

By the end of the morning every house on the block had a window box gay with bloom. It was a dramatic sight and it stirred something in the hearts of the people which might have remained forever dormant. But the seed was there. It needed only to be nurtured.

"It gives a lift to the heart just to look at it." said an elderly grandmother sitting on her door step.

"Don't it look countryfied!" exclaimed a young mother holding a child in her arms.

"It sure makes a difference!" said a man passing along the street.

Before the morning was over a group from Emily Street, just a block north of Mercy Street, came over to the Settlement to ask if their block could become a Garden Block, and late in the afternoon neighbors from two other blocks came to make the same request.

CALVARY SETTLEMENT

At Calvary Settlement in South Philadelphia the window boxes were made by the teen-age boys in the workshop. After they had been put up and filled with soil the boys, entirely on their own initiative, formed a Boy's Patrol to see that no harm came to the flowers and that the block was kept perfectly clean.

On the day designated for the planting of the flowers there was great excitement on the street. Steps were scrubbed, and the sidewalks were swept. Before the last box had been planted one of the women had gone around the corner and purchased a small can of paint and was on a step-ladder painting the woodwork around her door and windows. Later that day several other women on the block had followed her example, and when the men came home from work they took over, and vied with each other to see who could do the best job. This block was sponsored by The Garden Club of Philadelphia.

DIXON HOUSE

At the Settlement Houses which did not wish to undertake the planting of a Garden Block this first year, small adult and youth groups were organized, each group being sponsored by one of the suburban Garden Clubs.

At Dixon House the adult group was sponsored by the Hill and Hollow Garden Club. Several little back yards were planted and in the autumn each member received a lovely house plant. For a number of the members in the group it was the first plant they had ever had. One elderly woman who lived alone remarked to the Chairman of the Neighborhood Garden Association upon the occasion of one of her visits: "It's such company! It's just like a little boy. In the morning I puts it over here, then in the afternoon I moves it over here, so it will get the sun and be happy."

The junior girl group was sponsored by the Junior Providence Garden Club. Each girl received a box of plants for a tiny back yard garden and in the autumn each member received 6 paper-white narcissus bulbs with a container and pebbles and careful instructions for forcing them. They were in bloom at Christmas time and brought great joy to the children and their families.

The little girl group, which had chosen the name The Busy Bees, planted a border of spring flowering bulbs in the small recreational area at the rear of the Settlement House. Each member planted a section of the border and made a scrapbook containing a picture of each of the bulbs which she had cut out of a catalogue.

The following spring the bulbs were in bloom at Easter time and one of the little girls wrote in her scrapbook, "To me they are the most beautiful flowers in all the world because I was part of them being there."

UNITED NEIGHBORS SETTLEMENT

A number of little gardens were planted in back yards and in each box of plants brought in by the members of the Weeders Garden Club was a paper bag containing a dozen gladiolus bulbs. This was a delightful touch and brought great joy to the recipients.

WESTERN COMMUNITY HOUSE

At Western Community House three groups had been formed previously under the direction of Mrs. Elizabeth Forrester. One was a Golden Age group, another was a group of teen-age girls known as Just-Us-Girls and there was a younger group called the Golden Slipper group. These two Junior groups undertook the project of making the side yard of the Settlement beautiful with flower boxes and hanging brackets holding potted plants on the high board fence. These three groups were sponsored by the Germantown Garden Club. The sponsors brought in a wide variety of plants and took great interest in the project. In June a member of the sponsoring group invited the members of the Golden Age Club to visit her garden which was a never-to-be-forgotten pleasure. And in the autumn each member received paper-white narcissus bulbs to be forced into bloom for Christmas.

THE PUBLIC HOUSING PROJECT

THE RICHARD ALLEN HOMES

The Richard Allen Homes is a low rent public housing project for 1300 families.

SPONSORING GARDEN CLUBS

Bala-Cynwyd Garden Club	Old York Road Garden Club
Drexel Hill Garden Club	Providence Garden Club
Huntingdon Valley Garden Club	Springfield Garden Club
Lansdowne Garden Club	Wissahickon Garden Club

With the fine cooperation of Mr. Alton C. Berry, Manager, and Mrs. Ann Nichols, Home Advisor, a most successful garden project was carried out.

The slogan: "Make Richard Allen Homes the Garden Spot of North Philadelphia" was adopted and great enthusiasm resulted. The children were organized into a Richard Allen Homes Garden Patrol, with arm bands bearing this insignia.

The sponsoring Garden Clubs supplied plants for nearly 800 little door-yard garden plots and backyard gardens, and people came from far and near to admire the little gardens.

There was a little girl of ten who, when she learned that the plants would be brought in on a certain day, begged her mother to ask the teacher if she could be excused for the day so that she could help plant their garden, and the very wise teacher gave her consent. There was a little eleven year old boy who asked the Chairman of the Neighborhood Garden Association one day when she was visiting the project, if he could show her a special garden. As they stood admiring the garden he looked up at her and said "Every afternoon when I go over to the playground to swing I always come this way so that I can stand here for a few minutes and look at this garden."

All the gardens were judged during the late summer and those which had received good care were placed on the Honor Roll. Narcissus bulbs and tulip bulbs were awarded as prizes.

In September a flower show was held under the direction of the School of Horticulture at Ambler. It was the first time that anyone in the area had ever seen a flower show and it was a thrilling event for everyone.

ALEXANDER WILSON SCHOOL PROJECT

Miss Myrtle Glenn, Principal of the Alexander Wilson Elementary School in West Philadelphia, was one of the representatives present at the meeting on February 23rd when The Neighborhood Garden Association of Philadelphia was organized. Miss Glenn was receptive to the idea of having a pilot program initiated at her school and with the aid of her fine staff of teachers an excellent program was developed.

Special assembly programs were held. Songs about flowers were sung and poems about flowers and gardens were written by the children. Attractive posters were made, using pictures of flowers cut out of catalogues, and seedlings were started in little boxes on classroom window sills.

The private schools in and near Philadelphia were asked if their students would be interested in participating in this project. It was suggested that on a designated day in May each child bring to school a geranium plant in bloom. It was further suggested that parents having station wagons be asked to bring the plants to the Alexander Wilson School.

Six private schools volunteered to share in this program. The day when the plants would be brought in was eagerly awaited by the children in the Alexander Wilson School. At last it arrived. The boys in the Safety Patrol had the privilege of unloading the plants when the station wagons drove up, and placing them on a large table in the Assembly Hall. The mothers who had driven the station wagons and the class representatives from the private schools were invited to stay for the simple, impressive ceremony. After a few songs the children recited the pledge which they had prepared.

As a member of The Neighborhood Garden Association
I pledge to help keep my community clean and neat.
I further pledge to make my community more beautiful by planting flowers.
I shall protect my plants with good care and I shall never destroy or take my neighbor's plants or flowers.

18

Before

A back yard garden

Richard Allen Homes

A bare place

Made bright with bloom

A community garden

A plot of their own

The children then came forward, one by one, to receive one of the beautiful geraniums. To see the light in their faces as they returned to their seats was a never-to-be-forgotten experience to those in the audience who had the joy of making this project possible.

As a class-room program the children were taught how to make cuttings from their plants so that they could give a geranium to someone who had never known the joy of having a plant of his own.

AUTUMN MEETING

The autumn meeting of the Neighborhood Garden Association was held in October. Present at the meeting were the Committee members of the eighteen sponsoring Garden Clubs, the Directors of the Settlement Houses, the Home Advisor at the Richard Allen Housing Project and Miss Glenn, Principal of the Alexander Wilson School.

The Chairman of the Neighborhood Garden Association presented her report of the activities which had taken place during the spring and summer of 1953.

On the seven Garden Blocks 427 window boxes had been planted by the sponsoring Garden Clubs and, in spite of the many warnings and predictions by the sceptics, only one box had a plant taken from it. And no harm had come to any of the little gardens.

During this first year of endeavor the Neighborhood Garden Association had touched the lives of thousands of people in the blighted areas of the city, young and old. The youngest participant was a little boy of five who hauled soil from a vacant lot in his wagon to make a tiny garden beside the steps of the little frame house in which he lived at Front and Ellsworth Streets. The oldest participant was nearly ninety, a member of the Golden Age Club at Western Community House.

Miss Nicola, the Director of St. Martha's Settlement, spoke of the upsurge of pride which had followed the planting of the window boxes and reported that a number of blocks in her area had already made application to become a Garden Block next spring.

Miss Cramer, the Director of Calvary Settlement, told about the Public Health nurse who reported at a staff meeting that when she turned into the 2000 block on Ellsworth Street to visit a patient she had felt such an uplift of spirit for there were flower boxes at every window and the street was always clean.

All this was accomplished through the fine spirit of cooperation between the Settlement Houses and other agencies and the sponsoring groups—the Garden Clubs and private schools.

In North Philadelphia there were nearly 800 little gardens gay with bloom at the Richard Allen Public Housing Project.

In South Philadelphia hundreds of families on the seven Garden Blocks had lovely flower boxes at their windows, and in West Philadelphia there was a beautiful geranium on many a window sill or porch, lovingly tended by an eager child.

All this held a bright promise for what the future might be for the blighted areas of Philadelphia, and perhaps it heralds a return to William Penn's ideal of "a Greene Country Towne."

"It is one of the most beautiful compensations in this life, that no man can sincerely try to help another without helping himself."
—*Emerson*

A pleasant Garden Block

PLANS FOR THE SECOND YEAR

When the Neighborhood Garden Association Committee met in February, 1954 many matters were brought up for discussion.

A Report of Activities for 1953 had been printed in booklet form and was ready for distribution.

It was agreed that copies of the Report should be sent to all participating groups, and members of the Committee were asked to send in the names of people who might be interested in knowing more about the Neighborhood Garden Association program.

Everyone agreed that the Garden Blocks had been an outstanding success and had resulted in encouraging good neighborhood spirit on all of the seven blocks. It was therefore decided to put special emphasis on the organization of new Garden Blocks. Before the season was over thirty-four blocks in widely scattered parts of the city had become Garden Blocks and nearly two thousand window boxes had been planted by the sponsoring Garden Club groups.

Since by joining individual effort into a community of effort each person finds the sphere of his own efforts enlarged and strengthened, it was deemed wise, at the beginning of this second year, to ask the various groups at the Settlement Houses to form their own garden clubs. If certain requirements were met these new clubs would become member clubs of the Neighborhood Garden Association. One of the most important requirements was that the club must undertake some project for community improvement each year.

The suggestion was accepted with enthusiasm and twelve clubs were formed. Officers were elected, club names were chosen with great care and programs were planned with eagerness.

CALVARY SETTLEMENT

Early in the spring the Calvary Neighborhood Flower Club was organized and became a very active group. Monthly meetings were held at the Settlement House, and the Calvary Neighborhood Flower Club was one of the two clubs which qualified for the Award of Merit, a very high honor. The members of the club helped to organize several Garden Blocks in the area. At the Christmas meeting of the Club a demonstration of making wreaths and other decorations was given by Mrs. McNeill, one of the members of the Oasis Garden Club. These were used to trim the Settlement House and the homes of the club members.

DIXON HOUSE

At Dixon House the club which was organized on the 2000 block of Mountain Street chose the name Mountain Gardens. Because of the structure of the houses on this block it was impossible to have window boxes, but, quite undaunted by this, the members of the club secured for a modest sum some large tin tubs about eighteen inches in diameter. These were painted green, rubble was placed in the bottom for drainage, and the cans were then filled with soil. The plants were carefully selected by the sponsoring Garden Club and included wax begonias, fuchsias, impatiens and coleus for the shady side of the street and geraniums, lantana, marigolds and zinnias for the sunny side. The plants received good care and continued in bloom until late in the autumn, adding much color and beauty to the block. In December Christmas trees were planted in the tubs and through the generosity of the sponsoring club, the Junior Providence Garden Club, strings of lights were provided which made the block very festive and gay throughout the holiday season.

FRIENDS' NEIGHBORHOOD GUILD

The Garden Block organized by the Friends' Neighborhood Guild was an inter-racial block, Negro, Puerto Rican and white. It was a block which carried very heavy traffic, yet in spite of this hazard no vandalism was encountered. The Twin Valleys Garden Club was the sponsoring group and not only brought in an excellent selection of flowers, but also brought in a generous quatity of rich, composted soil which was a most valued contribution. It was a very dreary part of the city where flowers were seldom, if ever, seen and the people on the block took great pride and interest in their boxes.

UNITED NEIGHBORS SETTLEMENT

In the heart of Philadelphia there was an alley where conditions were so deplorable that it was hard to believe that it was almost within the shadow of City Hall. Opening off this alley was a little court where the residents, with the help of the United Neighbors Settlement, had striven to rise above the sordidness of their surroundings. It was known as Ken-Watt Court. Through the efforts of a member of the staff of the Settlement various improvements had been made and a Ken-Watt Community Club had been formed. Indoor plumbing had replaced the outside privies, the houses had been repaired and painted and they were ready for the next step. The staff worker who had seen some of the Garden Blocks suggested that they ask the Neighborhood Garden Association if they could become a Garden Court.

The Planters' Garden Club became the sponsors of this project, and working in close and enthusiastic cooperation with the people living in the court, they carried through a most outstanding program. The window boxes and ground boxes were made by the older boys and young men and the workmanship was of such high quality and the boxes so attractive, each box bearing the monogram of the club, that they became a model for other groups.

The plants were selected with care. For the ground boxes beside the doorways marigolds, zinnias, flowering tobacco and seedling dahlias were used. Against a blank wall on the left as one entered the court a long, low box was used with a rose trellis at each end. The transformation of that little court was a minor miracle.

On Planting Day the Chairman of the Neighborhood Garden Association lingered after the others had gone, and as she was leaving a red police car drew up in the alley and stopped. The police officer took one long look into the court. "Lady," he said, "you're just throwing your time and your money away. There won't be a thing left there in twenty-four hours."

"You may be mistaken," replied the Chairman.

"I ought to know, I've been on this beat for 17 years. This is one of the toughest parts of the whole city," he replied and drove off.

The following Sunday more than a hundred people came to visit Ken-Watt Court. Some of them had never even seen a flower. The next day the word Welcome was painted in large letters on the long flower box beside the blank wall. Upon one of her visits a resident of the court remarked to the Chairman,—"We don't have to go anywhere in the evening now. We have everything right here."

At the end of the season the staff worker from the Settlement held a meeting of the residents and he gave them a questionnaire to fill out. On the list were a number of things which had been accomplished—the repair of the houses, the whitewashing of all the outside walls, the installation of indoor plumbing, the flower boxes, the painting of the woodwork on the houses. The residents were asked to check the one which had given them the most satisfaction.

After he had glanced over the questionnaires and had found, to his amazement, that everyone had checked The Flowers, he turned to them and said, "Do you mean to tell me that you would put the flowers above your indoor plumbing in importance?"

Everyone nodded and said, "Yes, we would."

LEAGUE STREET

In another part of the city, very near the shore of the Delaware River, there is a little street so narrow that it is closed to all traffic. League Street is lined with quaint, little brick houses built in colonial days. This Garden Block project was sponsored by The Weeders Garden Club. The residents on the block are now largely Polish, and they were so enthusiastic over the flowers that there was 100 per cent participation within the block. As one side of the block was extremely shady it presented something of a problem, but this was taken into consideration by the sponsoring committee when selecting the plants and coleus, begonias and impatiens throve well even in the dense summer shade. The residents on the block formed The League Street Neighbors Association and became very active in planning for block improvement. It sponsored a festive Christmas party on December 22nd to bring its activities to a close.

SAINT MARTHA'S SETTLEMENT

Early in the spring six garden clubs were formed at St. Martha's Settlement House on the block basis. There was The Gardenia Garden Club on the 700 block of Mercy Street, and the Flower Silver Star Club on the 500 block of Cantrell Street, the Flower Garden Club on the 700 block of Winton Street, and there were two clubs on Emily Street.

The enthusiasm of these groups and the interest in the Garden Block program was most heartening. The first second-year block to be planted was the 700 block on Mercy Street. In the autumn of that year when the final check was made on the window boxes on the Garden Blocks two blocks had 100% on the Honor Roll. One of these was the 700 block of Mercy Street. All the other blocks in this area also had a high percent on the Honor Roll, which was proof of the excellent care which the flowers and boxes had received throughout the season.

WESTERN COMMUNITY HOUSE

Early in the year a group of four women had met with Mrs. Forrester at Western Community House to discuss the organization of a Garden Club. Careful thought was given to the selection of a name and at length it was decided to call it The Oasis Garden Club since one of the objectives was to make their community an oasis in the desert of the city. The Oasis Garden Club, in one year, grew from the four founding members to a membership of 282. The activities of this club have been outstanding and far-reaching. Monthly meetings were held at Western Community House and in the intervening period block meetings were held at the home of the Block Leader to discuss special block problems and measures for block improvement.

Under the enthusiastic sponsorship of the Germantown Garden Club and with the help of the Oasis Garden Club 12 Garden Block projects were undertaken. On two of these blocks little gardens were developed on vacant lots, 1500 Rodman Street and 1900 Naudain Street. And a story hour for the children was held twice a week in each of these gardens.

On the 30th of September the Oasis Garden Club held its first Flower Show. Flowers to be used by the exhibitors were brought in from the gardens of members of the Germantown Garden Club. There were 126 entries among the members of the Oasis Garden Club and prizes were awarded in five classes, special awards being given to the exhibitor scoring the most points and to the Block Leader whose block scored the most points.

KATER STREET

The 2100 block on Kater Street in the Western Community area was one of the few second year Garden Blocks to qualify for a high award. One day in early spring when the Chairman of the Neighborhood Garden Association was visiting the block the Leader said to her very eagerly, "I'm just ready for some new ideas!"

The suggestion was made that she ask her husband to make a small semi-circular brick bay between the two front windows in which a climbing

Attractive homes on a Garden Block

rose could be planted. The Chairman gave her full directions for building the bay and assured her that if the bay was built and filled with soil she would bring a rose bush for her to plant in it. Upon her next visit a few days later the bay had been built and filled with soil and a few days later she brought the rose bush which was in a large tarpaper pot. Together they planted it, measuring the depth of the hole needed and removing the tarpaper pot with the utmost care in order not to disturb the roots. On the bush there were several young, vigorous shoots and a number of buds almost ready to open. At last it was safely in its new home and it was soon surrounded by admiring neighbors, asking if they, too, could have a rose. The Chairman explained that she could give roses only to Garden Block Leaders, but that she could get roses for them at wholesale rates and would be glad to bring them in for anyone who had a bay ready for planting.

On the day her rose bush had a bud that was beginning to open the Block Leader was so fearful that someone might come by and pick it she sat by her window all night long. Fortunately no harm came to her precious rose.

Within the next few weeks 47 rose bays were built on the 2100 Kater block and each rose bush was planted with loving care. By the middle of June the entire block looked like a garden and people came from far and near to see it.

News travels quickly from block to block, and soon people of other blocks began to build rose bays and that whole section became famous for its roses.

Most surprising was the fact that the roses required no spraying. They were grade A stock and were completely free from any pests and diseases when they were brought in and continued to remain so.

WHARTON CENTER

The Garden Block project on the 1700 block of North Beechwood Street brought the work of the Association into an entirely new area of the city. A meeting was held at Wharton Center in March which was attended by several fathers and mothers and a few of the teen-agers from the Beechwood block. Pictures were shown of the projects in other parts of the city. There followed a discussion of the possibilities of organizing a Garden Block project on 1700 Beechwood Street. A staff worker at the Center, Mr. James Johnson, had a model window box on display. He asked for volunteers among the teen-age boys present to help build the window boxes, and with the assurance of their cooperation the project was launched. The boys worked industriously during the spring under Mr. Johnson's direction and 83 boxes were built, 71 for Beechwood Street and 12 for Wharton Center on North 22nd Street.

The day in May which was scheduled for the planting of the window boxes was cold and cheerless with a drizzly rain, and on that morning Beechwood Street presented a dreary aspect with its dilapidated fences, its gutters strewn with trash and garbage and its vacant lots filled with refuse.

The Chairman of the Neighborhood Garden Association and Mr. Johnson, the staff worker from Wharton Center, were present to welcome the members of the sponsoring committee from the Four Counties Garden Club, and the street soon came to life. The boys crowded around the station wagons to help unload the plants, and the women ventured out in spite of the drizzle, eager to receive the flowers for their window boxes, and the block was soon humming with activity. By noon the sun had come out and the last window box had been planted.

The women went up and down the street admiring each others' flowers. "This was the most dumpified place I ever had seen," said one woman to another. "Now it even smells good!"

Then a miracle happened on Beechwood Street. For the first time people on the block seemed to become aware of the trash and the squalor on every side. One of the men who had watched the planting of the boxes with considerable interest suddenly called over to a friend across the street, "Hi! Tom, let's clean the street!" Tom looked up and down the block. "It sure do need it, don't it," replied Tom. "O.K. let's get moving," replied the instigator of the idea. He disappeared for a moment and came out with a wrench and a hose.

"Come on everybody. Do your part!" he shouted as he attached the hose to the fire hydrant and turned the water on.

Out came the brooms and the shovels and it seemed as if every man, woman, and child had become a self-appointed member of the Street Cleaning Department and was helping to clean the block. The side walks were swept off, the steps were scrubbed. One woman got a can of paint and painted the woodwork around her cellar window. One woman went from door to door collecting money to buy a special kind of paint to make the curb white. "Anybody," she said, "would be willing to chip in 25¢ to help a street that looks like this with the flowers on it." And a group of teen-age boys, when they came home from school, set out to white-wash a long, shabby fence in front of a vacant lot.

And the younger children were not forgotten. One of the greatest longings in the heart of a child living in the crowded conditions of the ghetto is for something which is his or her very own. But when a house built originally for one family, as were the houses on Beechwood Street, later becomes divided into six two-room apartments there is very little chance of having something you could really call your own.

With the aid of Mr. Johnson, we had been able to get a list giving the age of every child between six and twelve on the block. The girls in the Social Service Club at the School of Horticulture in Ambler were asked if they would like to bring in on the day the window boxes were planted something suitable for the children.

One of the girls had the clever idea of taking No. 10 juice cans, turning them on their side and cutting a large piece out of the top. The cans were painted green and on the front of each can were the initials of one of the children. Here, at last was something that the child could call his own. He could prove it! His or her initials were on it! The cans were filled with soil and planted with dwarf marigolds and ageratum and other low growing flowers.

When the students brought these little "fences boxes," as they called them, in on the afternoon of Planting Day they were hung on the board fences, according to family, and each one was placed at eye level for the child whose initials were on it. It was an exciting moment for the children and for the grown-ups, too. In the face of everyone on the block there was a glow of joy and pride as they surveyed their block, so swept and clean, and their beautiful flower boxes and the little fence boxes.

At the end of the afternoon Mr. Johnson turned to the Chairman of the Neighborhood Garden Association and said with deep feeling, "Nothing, absolutely nothing, could have done for this block what these flowers have done! For the first time the people have overcome their apathy. For the first time neighbors have learned to work together."

Nor was the enthusiasm short-lived. Throughout the summer the people on Beechwood Street held weekly rummage sales to raise money for block improvement. The largest of the vacant lots was cleaned up and the money which was raised was used to buy playground equipment for the children.

When Mr. Johnson returned to the Wharton Center on the afternoon of Planting Day he found that twelve people had come to the Center from Norwood Street during the day to ask if their block could become a Garden Block. It was actually late in June before this project got under way, but when Planting Day finally came a committee from Beechwood Street went over to Norwood Street, one block away, to show them how to plant their boxes, another happy example of neighbors helping neighbors.

A few weeks later the Neighborhood Garden Association received a letter from Mr. Johnson, reporting progress on Beechwood Street. The letter closed with the following paragraph:

"The Neighborhood Garden Association has given to the darkened area of Philadelphia a brilliant beacon of light to guide their steps to better ways of living."

A dreary block

Beechwood Street

The first planting day

The afternoon clean-up

Fence boxes for the children

The block one year later

RICHARD ALLEN HOMES PROJECT

Under the leadership of Mrs. Nichols, the Home Advisor, two very active junior Garden Clubs were organized at the Richard Allen Homes, the Daisy Garden Club and the Rose Marie Garden Club.

The Upper Dublin 4-H Club in the suburbs undertook as one of their projects the growing of plants for these two clubs. Each member of the 4-H Club grew 10 tom-thumb flats containing twelve plants each. When the plants were in bloom a committee from the 4-H Club took them in to the Richard Allen Homes. They took tools with them and helped the boys and girls prepare the garden beds and plant the flowers, an experience which was enjoyed by both groups.

The sponsoring Garden Clubs were again very active and brought in the flowers for the little dooryard gardens which received affectionate care throughout the season. In the autumn one of the Garden Clubs brought in 200 tulip bulbs which were planted for spring bloom. Another club brought in a generous quantity of perennials for fall planting, and one group brought in a collection of beautiful house plants which were distributed among the elderly and the shut-ins. These were so gratefully received that in December the members brought in a large number of attractive containers in which paper-white narcissus had been started. These were in bloom at Christmas time and brought joy and cheer to many.

ALEXANDER WILSON SCHOOL PROJECT

The project undertaken was the planting of a Demonstration Garden Block on S. 46th Street to show how attractive a city block could be made through the use of flowers.

The project was sponsored by the children in the private schools in the Philadelphia area and the students from the School of Horticulture at Ambler, assisted by the boys in the Safety Patrol at the Alexander Wilson School.

On Planting Day, May 17th, the children in the private schools brought flowering plants to school, a geranium, a petunia, a begonia, an impatiens

A Garden Block in South Philadelphia

"No ray of sunlight is ever lost,
but the green which it awakens into existence needs time to sprout,
and it is not always granted to the sower to see the harvest.
"All work that is worth anything is done in faith."
—*Albert Schweitzer*

or a verbena. These were brought to the Alexander Wilson School, in most cases, by representatives from the participating classes.

The planting was done under the direction of the Horticultural students, assisted by the Safety Patrol boys.

Before the end of the day 68 porch boxes and 32 little dooryard gardens had been planted, and the block was gay with bloom and beauty.

In order that the project might be more meaningful for their students, some of the private schools brought groups to see the street before the planting was done, and again after it had been completed, and the children have come to speak of it as "Our Block."

The Demonstration Block proved such an inspiration to the surrounding community that the neighbors in two nearby blocks organized similar projects.

One of the little boys living on the Demonstration Block wrote a letter to the Neighborhood Garden Association. It was brief and very sincere.

"Thank you for making our block a wonderful sight to look at. It makes me feel real good inside."

RECOGNITION NIGHT DINNER

The first Recognition Night Dinner of the Neighborhood Garden Association was held on November 4th at the Marion Anderson Recreation Center. All participating groups were represented,—the sponsoring Garden Clubs, the Settlement Houses and other agencies and every Garden Block. It was a tremendously interesting and inspiring occasion.

Each Garden Block Leader gave a report, telling what had been accomplished on his or her block. The Honor Roll awards were presented to the Block Leaders to be distributed by them to each person on the Honor Roll. The award was a bag containing paper-white narcissus bulbs and bulb fiber with directions for growing bulbs indoors.

Nine Blocks qualified for the Award of Merit in recognition of one year of outstanding achievement. Three Junior Garden Clubs also received Awards.

Two second-year Garden Blocks, 2100 Kater Street and 2000 Ellsworth Street, received the highest Award of Merit,—a tree to be planted on their block. The requirements for this award were: a minimum of two years of constructive effort, a high percentage of participation within the block, good standards in keeping the block clean, a high percentage of participants on the Honor Roll and a definite project for community improvement.

One Block Leader in giving her report told of the fine spirit of cooperation in her block, and she spoke of the little garden they had made on a vacant lot, and of the supper which had been held to raise money for block improvement. And she ended by saying, "A year ago we didn't even know each other to speak to by name, and now we are all neighbors working together."

At the meeting of the Neighborhood Garden Association Committee in February, 1955, everyone agreed that the Neighborhood Garden Association had developed a unique program which had great potentials.

During the past season delegations from Baltimore, Brooklyn and Washington had come to see Philadelphia's Garden Blocks and, by previous arrangement, had been taken on guided tours. Requests for information concerning the program had been received from many other communities. Many lectures had been given to local groups, and in January the Chairman of the Association had been invited by The Garden Club of Cleveland to give an illustrated lecture on the Garden Block Program, in the hope that Cleveland would start a similar project.

In the collection of slides which had been taken there were pictures of each block before any improvement had been undertaken, pictures taken during Planting Day and others taken at later periods. These slides, all in color, tell a very vivid and convincing story and are a tremendous asset to the Association.

At this winter meeting in February it was felt that the time had come to have a lawyer, in consultation with members of the Committee, prepare a Constitution and By-Laws for the Association. A motion was made, seconded and passed that this be done.

When completed a copy of the Constitution and the By-Laws was sent to each member of the Committee and at the April meeting received a final vote of acceptance.

It was a busy spring for the Neighborhood Garden Association. During the month of May 36 new Garden Blocks and 27 second year blocks were planted:—a total of 63 blocks with more than 2,800 window boxes.

It was decided to ask each Garden Block Leader to form a Welcoming Committee to be present on Planting Day to greet the members of the Sponsoring Garden Club Committee and help with the unloading of the plants. An attractive white ribbon bearing the word COMMITTEE in gold letters would be supplied by the Association for each member of the Welcoming Committee.

A new form was adopted in sending out Planting Day Confirmations to the Chairmen of the sponsoring Committees, the Block Leaders and the Settlement Houses (if such an agency was involved). The new form is shown here.

A TYPICAL PLANTING DAY CONFIRMATION

Name of Sponsoring Garden Club
    Name of Chairman of Sponsoring Club Committee
    Address of Chairman   Telephone Number

Garden Block Leader
    Name of Leader
    Address of Leader   Telephone Number

Planting Date:

    Hour:

Number of Window Boxes

Directions for reaching the Garden Block
    Give complete details

Copy of Confirmation sent to:
    Chairman of The Neighborhood Garden Association
    Chairman of the Garden Club Sponsoring Committee
    Garden Block Leader

THE SETTLEMENTS

CALVARY SETTLEMENT

During the spring of 1955 a beautiful little garden was developed on a vacant lot on Annin Street, just at the rear of the Settlement House.

Tools were borrowed from a kindly contractor and on a designated Saturday the men and boys on the block turned in and, under supervision, leveled off the ground, staked out the beds and put up the fence which had been delivered the previous day. During the week a large load of top soil and a load of bricks were delivered and by the end of the following Saturday the beds were ready for planting.

The members of the sponsoring Club, The Garden Club of Philadelphia, brought in the plant materials;—climbing roses to be planted along the fence and trained on lattices against the wall of the adjoining house and on the arbor. And there were other plants, carefully selected perennials and shrubs.

When the roses were in bloom in June many visitors came to see and enjoy the garden. One woman who had heard about the garden had walked two miles to see it. The Chairman of the Neighborhood Garden Association happened to be the only person in the garden at the time. She greeted the visitor and answered some of her eager questions. When the visitor was about to go she stood for a few moments beside the flower border and then turned to the Chairman. "Oh! the roses are *so* beautiful," she said softly. "It makes me feel like kneeling down." At the gate she turned and came back. "We have a vacant lot on my block. Do you think it could ever look like this?" She left her name and address with the Chairman who promised to stop and look at the vacant lot on her block.

The joy which Miss Cramer, the Director of the Calvary Settlement, took in the garden was a delight to see. It was named The Dream Garden, for it was, indeed, a dream come true.

WESTERN COMMUNITY HOUSE

THE SECRET GARDEN. On one of the Garden Blocks, 1500 Rodman Street, there was a vacant lot, and behind the high board fence which shielded the lot from the street a minor miracle took place. In January 1955 the Block

A block near Center City before

Leader and two neighbors decided that they would like to make a little garden on this lot which, through the years, had become trash filled. Undaunted
by the task before them, the three women slipped into the lot through a back
alley at night and loaded their baskets, placing them along the sidewalk on
trash collection days. At last after nearly three months, the lot was cleared
and the three neighbors began to work on the garden. They made little borders along the sides, edging them with bricks which they had saved from the
rubble, and they planted scarlet runner beans against the walls, training them
up on strings. They repaired and painted the dilapidated fence at the rear
of the lot, and in the center of the garden they made a round flower bed,
edged with white-washed bricks.

They called it the "Secret Garden" because no one even suspected that anything was going on behind the high board fence along the street until the garden was, at length, completed. Then the high board fence was taken down, and was replaced with a little white picket fence and gate, made by the husband of the Chairman of the Germantown Garden Club Committee.

Benches were placed in the garden and it became a pleasant gathering place for neighbors on summer afternoons and evenings. A meeting of the Oasis Garden Club was held in the Garden in August, the members all joining in the lovely Neighborhood Garden Association hymn, "God Who Toucheth Earth with Beauty," as the meeting came to a close at twilight. At Christmas time the tree, which had been awarded to the block for two years of constructive work, was placed in the Secret Garden where all could enjoy it, and on Christmas Eve the people on the block gathered around to sing Christmas carols. This took place on a block where a year before the neighbors had not known each other well enough to speak to by name.

The following June the Chairman of the Association, on one of her periodic visits to the area, stopped to see the Secret Garden. One of the

Entrance to Secret Garden

View of Garden

Garden becomes a center of the community

women who had been a member of the original group was on her knees cultivating a garden bed. They chatted together for a few minutes and then she got up and came over to the little picket fence. She stood there, silent for a time, and then, addressing the Chairman by name, she said in a very hesitating way: "When you are working in a garden it makes you feel sort of close to God, doesn't it?" How wonderful it was for her to be able to make that discovery in one of the most congested areas in the city!

Under the guidance of Mrs. Forrester, Program Director at Western Community House, the Oasis Garden Club had become a vital force for community betterment. The Club was organized in 1954 as a member club of the Neighborhood Garden Association. In 1955 it drew up a constitution and by-laws, stating its purposes.

1. To improve living conditions in the home and neighborhood through the development of window box, vacant lot and backyard gardens.
2. To organize neighbors on the block and neighborhood level, creating an awareness in them of the importance of group action for better housing, street lights, and other changes they wish to bring about.
3. To strengthen family life by bringing beauty into the home and creating an interest in a delightful hobby which every member of the family can enjoy.
4. To help parents to guide their children into assuming responsibility not only for themselves, but for the community.

A letter from the Director of Western Community House:

I am sure that every social worker and every person interested in people must feel appalled and a bit over-powered when they visit, work or move into a community like our neighborhood. Yet I am equally certain that we dream of rising above the poverty and dirt that people seem to adjust themselves to.

It is difficult to express the apathy of people who, of a necessity, must live in such conditions. . . . Most of all we search for a handle for our dreams.

The Neighborhood Garden Association has done a miraculous deed in giving neighbors a handle by which they may grasp the dream. Your idea has paved the way for people to feel some concern and, we feel our neighbors are beginning to take a firm hold of their boot straps and one day our neighborhood will be a clean and proud one where the brotherly love and "greene towne" concepts will be real.

In all humility
Thomas H. Buress 3rd

When, in the spring of 1955, Mrs. Herd, a 74-year-old member of the Oasis Garden Club, moved to another area she took her love of flowers with her. She promptly put her Oasis Garden Club membership card in her window and urged everyone on the block to put up window boxes and get ready for Planting Day. When they asked about the flowers she assured them that they would be brought in on a certain date. As the day drew near the people kept asking her if she knew for sure that the flowers would come, and she began to feel a little anxious. Suppose they didn't come! When the appointed day came and the members of the sponsoring Garden Club Committee arrived and the Chairman of the Neighborhood Garden Association arrived with her car full of flowers Mrs. Herd almost wept with joy. She went up and down the block saying: "I told you they would come! I told you they would come!" Her anxieties were over. Her new neighbors were being shown how to take the plants out of the pots and how to plant them in their boxes, and by noon the block was gay with bloom and beauty.

The Chairman stayed after the Garden Club members had left to talk with Mrs. Herd and together they rejoiced over the change in the appearance of the block. Suddenly Mrs. Herd turned to her and said: "I go to bed thinking about flowers. I wake up thinking about flowers. I have flowers on my mind." There was a radiance in her face as she spoke.

WHARTON CENTER

In the early months of 1954 the block on N. Beechwood Street was typical of many other blocks in the area. It was a dismal, dreary street where nothing but apathy existed among the people living on it.

In the spring of 1955, at the time of its second Planting Day, Beechwood Street presented a very different appearance. The Beechwood Improvement Association had been formed by the people on the block, and under the leadership of Mr. Johnson, the Staff worker from Wharton Center, and the assistance of Mrs. Winston, the Block Leader, much had been accomplished. The trash-strewn vacant lots had been cleaned up, the woodwork on many of the houses had been painted, landlords had been willing to make improvements because of the change in the attitude of the tenants, and there was a feeling of civic pride among the residents on the block which had never existed before.

In June a three week vacation Bible School was held on a vacant lot in the block which a year before had ben covered with rubbish. And later in the summer four Story Hours were held through the courtesy of the branch Public Library.

During the summer the Oasis Garden Club, formed at Western Community House, invited a group from Wharton Center to visit some of the

MADISON COUNTY LIBRARY
CANTON, MISS. 39046

Garden Blocks in their area. It was a thrilling and eye-opening experience for this group, and they returned filled with enthusiasm. "We want to make our block look like the 2100 Kater Block!" one of them exclaimed. As they looked around they began to see the possibilities on their own block.

On Norwood Street, which had also become a Garden Block the year before, the men had organized a Club and devoted many hours to painting the woodwork on the houses, the landlords agreeing to supply the paint.

Early in the summer another block made application to become a Garden Block, and a sponsoring Garden Club was assigned to it. The Block Leader, who made the application, was blind. She was a remarkable person and became one of our most outstanding block leaders. Under her leadership the 2000 block on N. Woodstock Street became an award block.

"When one thinks of all the people on this street what has eyes and couldn't see what needed to be done, and it took a blind woman to lead them!" said one of the residents.

A block near Center City after

ALEXANDER WILSON SCHOOL PROJECT

Due to the generous participation on the part of ten private schools it was possible to expand the program and several new Garden Blocks were planted.

A very active Garden Club has been organized on the 1300 block of S. 46th Street, the block on which the school is located. The club has chosen the name "The Cheerful Garden Club", and under the able leadership of its president, Mrs. George Ware, much was accomplished.

The Christmas tree which was received as an Award of Merit from the Neighborhood Garden Association was placed at the end of the street and the entire area was beautifully decorated for the Christmas season.

RICHARD ALLEN HOMES

Several new Junior Garden Clubs have been formed and the members are taking a very active interest in their little gardens. A small piece of fenced in ground was available in one of the areas and the Old York Road Garden Club, under the able chairmanship of Mrs. Rheiner, developed a beautiful little garden on this plot. The garden was lovingly cared for by the little girls in the Rose-Marie Garden Club and throughout the season it was a source of joy to the many residents in the area.

Upon one of her visits to the garden the Chairman of the Neighborhood Garden Association was asked by one of the mothers: "Is my little girl too young to join the Garden Club? She's ten. I think it sort of keeps your mind clean to work with nature and flowers."

This same thought was expressed nearly four hundred years ago by John Gerard in his great Herbal.

Floures through their beatuy do bring to a liberall and gentle manly minde, the remembrance of honestie, comelinesse, and all kind of vertues. For it would be an unseembly thing for him who doth look upon and handle faire and beautiful things, and who frequenteth and is conversant in faire and beautiful places, to have his minde not faire.

From the Herbal of John Gerard, published in 1597

THE ANNUAL DINNER

The second Annual Dinner was held at the Marian Anderson Recreation Center on November 10th. Despite bad weather the room was filled to the limit of its capacity. All the sponsoring Garden Clubs, the Settlement Houses and other cooperating agencies, and every Garden Block were represented. Among the guests of honor were Miss Lilly Peck, Executive Secretary of the National Federation of Settlements, and Mrs. Lois Mattox Miller, of the Editorial Staff of the Readers' Digest.

The Hostess Clubs were the Calvary Flower Club and the Oasis Garden Club.

Reports were given by the Block Leaders and Certificates of Merit were awarded to fifteen blocks for two years or more of outstanding achievement, each block receiving a beautiful Christmas tree. Eight blocks received certificates for one year of constructive effort.

Special Citations were awarded to Miss Frances Cramer, Director of Calvary Settlement, Mrs. Elizabeth Forrester, Program Director at Western Community House, Mrs. Ann P. Nichols, Home Advisor at the Richard Allen Homes, Mr. James R. Johnson of Wharton Center, and Mrs. Betty Maston, Block Leader on 2100 Kater Street.

Slides of the Garden Blocks were shown and the program closed with the Neighborhood Garden Association hymn.

CHRISTMAS WORK SHOPS

The Christmas Work Shops held at a number of the Settlement Houses were such a success that it is hoped that they will spread widely throughout the city.

One was held in the United Neighbors' area at Southwark House under the sponsorship of the Junior League Garden Club, the Hill and Hollow Garden Club, the Planters, The Weeders and the Willowburn Garden Clubs.

Another Work Shop was held at St. Martha's Settlement, being sponsored by The Gardeners. In the five blocks in this area there was a lovely swag of evergreens, trimmed with gay ribbons and bells, on every door. It was a great contrast to the surrounding blocks where there was not a suggestion of greenery.

As one woman was leaving St. Martha's Settlement with her swag she held it out in her hands and looked at it. "Isn't it beautiful." she said very softly. "And I made it!" It was the first time in her life that she had created something which was beautiful, and her face was radiant with joy.

RECOGNITION

In January, 1956, The Neighborhood Garden Association of Philadelphia received a significant recognition. Its Chairman, Mrs. James Bush-Brown, became the twenty-third recipient of the Annual Philadelphia Gimbel Award.

There were more than 800 guests at the Award Luncheon on the eleventh of January. Mayor Dilworth, one of the guests of honor, gave an inspiring address which was followed by a slide presentation, showing before and after pictures of the Garden Blocks and the vacant lot gardens.

Mr. Arthur C. Kaufmann, Executive Head of Gimbels, asked Mrs. Bush-Brown to come forward to receive the Award and he then read the citation.

"As an educator, author, lecturer, civic leader and founder of The Neighborhood Garden Association of Philadelphia, she brought the spiritual gift of beauty to replace hopeless blight through her inspired idea of neighbors working together to make homes and communities places of dignity and pride."

The beautiful, hand-lettered Citation and a check for one thousand dollars, used to further the work of the Association, were then presented to Mrs. Bush-Brown.

"In accepting this Award," she said, "my heart is touched with humility, as I feel that it is an honor which belongs not to one person, but to all those who have worked with such diligence and zeal to make possible the development of our Garden Block program in the city of Philadelphia:—the garden clubs whose members have given so generously of their time, their knowledge and their skills, the Settlements and Community Centers whose staff workers have made such an important contribution to our program, and our fine Garden Block Leaders who have done so much to inspire the people on their blocks.

"It is through the cooperative efforts of all these groups, working in happy association with each other, that the Neighborhood Garden Association program has been so rewarding to all those whose lives it has touched.

"We have found that flowers speak to the heart, and, as the blocks which we have helped have become transformed with bloom and beauty, we have watched with reverence the growth of the spiritual fruits of our endeavors.

"The touches of beauty brought into these dreary, blighted areas have fallen like dew upon ground long parched by drought, and have stirred something within the hearts of the people which might have remained forever dormant. And out of this flowering of the spirit have grown a sense of individual dignity and worth, an enlightened vision and a faith that much may be accomplished when neighbors work together to improve their communities."

CONTINUING GROWTH

In 1956 the Annual Meeting of the Neighborhood Garden Association was held on the 23rd of February, which was the third anniversary of the founding of the Association.

We recalled our deep concern over the fact that we might meet nothing but apathy on the part of the people on the blocks, and that vandalism might prove to be such a hazard that the program would be doomed to failure.

Fortunately not a single instance of vandalism had been encountered. In every area we had met a most heart-warming response, and we realized that our faith in undertaking the Garden Block program had been more than justified.

The rapid increase in the number of Garden Blocks had far exceeded our expectation.

1953	7 Garden Blocks	1955	63 Garden Blocks
1954	34 Garden Blocks	1956	93 Garden Blocks

As we were planting on one of the blocks a staff worker from a Settlement House remarked to the Chairman of the Association: "It isn't only the flowers. It is what it has done to the hearts of the people. That is what makes it so wonderful!"

And those of us who had worked closely with the program during those first three years felt that this was very true. There was an acceptance of the responsibilities of good citizenship, a concern for the appearance of the street, a deepening concern for the welfare of the children, as evidenced by the organization of Play Streets and Story Hours, and Block Parties with square dancing in the roped off streets. And on several blocks there was the spontaneous organization of Young Mother's' Clubs.

One of the highlights of the year was the Philadelphia Flower Show in March.

Through the generosity of the Flower Show Officials, letters were given to the Staff Members from the Settlement Houses providing for free admission for people from the Garden Blocks when accompanied by a Staff member.

Never before had the Garden Block members had such a thrill! For most of them it was a new and very wonderful experience and every moment they spent at the Flower Show was precious to them.

They returned to their blocks filled with enthusiasm and with many new ideas for little front yard gardens and for small patios in their back yards and for turning vacant lots into delightful little gardens.

As they were gathering to leave the Flower Show one of the Garden Block Leaders turned to the Chairman of the Association and said, very reverently, "When I walked down that central aisle with all that beauty on every side around me I felt that I was walking hand in hand with God."

During the year 1956 there were six vacant lots on our Garden Blocks which became lovely gardens or play lots.

Cleaning the lot

WESTERN COMMUNITY AREA

The 1700 block on Rodman Street had been sponsored for two years by the Huntingdon Valley Garden Club. The people on the block had seen and admired the Secret Garden just two blocks away and they decided that they would like to have a garden on a vacant lot on their block.

Mrs. Edward L. Elliott and Mrs. George R. Haines, Co-Chairmen of the Sponsoring Committee, were enthusiastic over the idea, and developed a design which resulted in a garden of great charm.

On a Saturday morning in early spring the boys and men on the block cleared the lot of trash and the women loaded it into baskets and put it out on the curb for trash collection day. After the leveling of the lot had been completed the men built the low brick wall along the front of the lot with a low picket fence on the top of it. The beds were then laid out and made ready for planting. There was a wide central panel paved with gravel, with a

A trash-filled lot becomes a garden

Three weeks later. The Four Seasons Garden

pleasant sitting area at the far end. Carefully selected evergreen and flowering shrubs and a few climbing roses were planted against the walls of the
two adjacent houses and on a raised bed at the rear there was a lovely living
Christmas tree.

The people on the block named it the Four Seasons Garden because
it was so lovely at all seasons of the year.

A few days after the garden had been completed the little boys on the block between seven and eleven years of age formed a Club. At the first meeting of the Club, which was held in the garden, they made each boy stand up and say a few Bible verses. Only one boy succeeded without stumbling and he was promptly elected Chaplain of the Club. Each meeting was opened with a few Bible verses by the Chaplain. The Four Seasons Garden soon became a pleasant place for people on the block to sit on during long summer afternoons and many little social gatherings were held there.

During the summer Mayor Dilworth asked the Chairman of the Association if he could be taken on a tour of some of the Garden Blocks, and a date for the trip was arranged, and it was agreed that there would be no advance publicity. During the next week the Chairman drove through the blocks, as she often did, and stopped to chat with the Block Leader and others on the block. Before she left she mentioned very casually to the Block Leader that she might be coming through again with a friend on a certain day and hoped that she would be at home.

When she came to 1700 Rodman Street with its lovely Four Seasons Garden, the Block Leader replied, "Did you ever come through when I wasn't here? I never go off the block, from one year's end to another."

The day came for the tour and when they reached the 1700 Block of Rodman Street the Chairman left the car for a moment to let the Block Leader know that she was there. To her utter amazement she found that the Block Leader was not there. "She had to step off on some business," her teenage daughter explained.

On her way home the Block Leader was met by four of her children who told her that the Mayor had been on the block and that she had missed him.

A few days later when the Chairman drove through to tell her how sorry she was not to have found her at home the Leader said "I wrote him a letter. I told him to come again!"

On the 1500 block on Naudain Street another garden was made by the children on the block under the guidance of Mrs. F. Joseph Stokes, Jr., a member of the Sponsoring Committee of the Germantown Garden Club. The boys and girls worked earnestly in clearing the lot of trash and getting it ready for planting and it was gay and colorful, and many jolly block parties were held there.

Several blocks away there was a vacant lot on another Garden Block. On this block lived a little eleven year old girl named Shirley Halliday, and in her heart there was a longing to have a garden on that trash-filled lot near her home—a garden with a swinging gate.

The vacant lot

A little girl with a dream

Filled with determination, she organized the 17 little boys on her block into a clean-up squad, and they cleared the lot of trash. They were ready then for the next step, but there was no sponsoring group available to give them the help they needed.

Just at this crucial time a telephone call was received by the Chairman of the Association from a member of a small church group in Chester Valley, some thirty miles from Philadelphia, asking if they could become sponsors of a project. The following day they came in to see the lot on 1900 Kater Street.

They explained that they had been working on the restoration of a small church in Chester Valley, and as that work had now been completed they wanted to be of service to some other group.

They were an ideal sponsoring group for this particular project and they were enthusiastic over the opportunity. Plans for the little garden were drawn up, lumber for the fence was ordered and they came in and helped the boys build the fence. The garden beds were laid out, bricks were laid in the sitting area and a load of top soil was delivered. On the day that the soil was shovelled into the beds we ran out of soil. As the shrubs and perennials were to be brought in the following day it was a real emergency.

"Where can I go and get some soil here in the city?" asked Mrs. Dawes, the Chairman of the sponsoring committee. She had driven in with her ¼ ton farm truck filled with shovels and spading forks.

"Oh! You won't be able to get any soil here in the city, you would have to go out into the country," replied the Chairman.

"But I haven't time to go out into the country!" she said. Then, pausing for a moment, she turned to the boys who were raking the soil which had been put into the beds.

Her helpers

"Come on boys, get into my truck. We'll get some soil somewhere," she said. With shouts of joy the boys clambered into the little truck and off they drove.

"She won't come back until she has it," said one of the members of the sponsoring committee.

An hour and a half later they drove up Kater Street, triumphant. The boys were standing on top of a pile of soil beating out a tattoo on the roof of the truck. Never had they had such fun!

"Where did you get that soil?" asked the Chairman in utter amazement.

"Out where they are bull-dozing for the new expressway," replied Mrs. Dawes. "There was a big pile there and I asked a policeman if I could have some of it. He shook his head and said 'Oh no, lady, I can't let you do that.' Then I told him that we were a church group and that we were helping these children make a garden on a vacant lot in the city. I think that church was the magic word, for he said 'Well, if it is for a church I'll have to let you do it,' whereupon the boys leaped out of the truck and got to work with their shovels."

The plants were brought in the following day, shrubs, climbing roses in tar paper pots, and quantities of lovely annuals in bloom. The planting of the flowers was a wonderful experience for the children and before the afternoon was over people passing along the street were stopping to exclaim over the beauty of the little garden. And best of all, the garden had a swinging gate to delight the heart of every child. Shirley Halliday's dream had come true.

The men in the parish of St. Andrew's Church made a sand box of ample size and brought it in, and later there was a gift of a small playhouse.

On many a summer day the little girls made sandwiches and put up cold drinks and had their lunches in the garden. One of the little girls exclaimed to the Chairman when she was telling her about their picnics there "It's just like living in the country!"

During the month of May 29 Garden Blocks were planted in the Western Community House area. A total of 804 families, averaging 5 members per family, participated in the program and the 1,250 window boxes and flower bays were gay with bloom until late in the autumn.

The Oasis Garden Club held regular monthly meetings at Western Community House with many interesting programs.

The Annual Flower Show, sponsored by the Oasis Garden Club, was held on September 27th, and it was an outstanding event. There were 119 entries. The exhibitors ranged in age from five years to 76 years. Prizes were awarded and the greatest number of points was won by the 1700 Addison Garden Block.

The garden completed

"No great plan is ever carried out without meeting
and overcoming endless obstacles that try the skill of man's hand,
the quality of his courage, and the endurance of his faith."
—*Donald W. Douglas*

WHARTON CENTER AREA

The Four Counties Garden Club had sponsored the 1700 Beechwood block for two years, and it had then become an Independent Block.

There had been such improvement in the appearance of the block and the residents, having had an opportunity to see some of the lovely vacant lot gardens on blocks in other areas, were so eager to have a flower garden on one of the lots which had been cleared on Beechwood Street, that the Four Counties Club volunteered to help them.

Under the able Co-Chairmanship of Mrs. Clinton H. Brown and Mrs. Charles S. Truitt a garden of great charm was developed. The garden was enclosed along the front by a picket fence. The gate opened upon a wide gravel path leading to a pleasant sitting area at the rear. An attractive planting of flowering and evergreen shrubs was made, with low growing flowers along the edge of the path. It was a very inviting garden and many of the older residents on the block found it a delightful place to sit on summer afternoons.

A few weeks after the garden had been completed the young girls on the block formed a Club called The Echoes. All their meetings and many little social events which they organized were held in the garden.

This was the first vacant lot garden in the North Philadelphia area. Word quickly spread from block to block and many neighbors came to see and admire this lovely little garden, and went home with the thought that perhaps someday they, too, could have a garden on their own block.

After the flower garden had been completed the residents on the block, entirely on their own initiative, took down the high board fences in front of three other vacant lots on the street, cleared away the trash, rebuilt the fences to a height of about three and a half feet. They then made long flower boxes, skillfully fastened them to the top of the fences and filled them with flowers. One lot was used as a play lot for little children, another for older boys and girls and the third, which was a lot of larger size, was used by teenagers and adults for more active sports.

Hundreds of children shared the use of these new play lots during the summer for games, story hours, parties and creative play.

SAINT MARTHA'S AREA

Remarkable progress was made during 1956 at Saint Martha's Settlement under the wise and stimulating guidance of Mrs. Bertha Corbin, the new staff worker.

Early in the spring a resident on the 1700 N. Norwood Garden Block offered to go down to St. Martha's and show the people there how to build their rose bays. As a result of his visit rose bays were built on Mercy, Emily and Cantrell Streets. On the scheduled Planting Day they were ready for the roses which were brought in by The Gardeners' Sponsoring Committee.

The roses bloomed well, the window boxes were colorful and gay throughout the summmer, the streets were kept clean, and many visitors came to see and enjoy the beauty of this South Philadelphia area. An account of these Garden Blocks at St. Martha's Settlement appeared in the Philadelphia Evening Bulletin.

The many local Garden Clubs which had been formed in this area held joint meetings each month at St. Martha's House and had many interesting programs. A Garden Club Newsletter was issued regularly by Mrs. Corbin, the new staff worker.

ALEXANDER WILSON SCHOOL AREA

After being sponsored for two years the 1300 block on S. 46th Street had become an Independent Block. Early in the spring the Cheerful Garden Club gave a dinner, each member of the Club contributing some tasty dish which she had made. The dinner was a great success and enough money was raised through this effort to purchase flowers for all the window boxes and porch boxes on the block. The street was again beautifully decorated at Christmas time.

At the Autumn Meeting of the Neighborhood Garden Association a staff member from one of the Settlement Houses mentioned in his report that the Garden Block program had created a fine sense of pride shared by the residents in the block and had resulted in better community relations. Another staff worker mentioned how meaningful our Garden Block program had been in fostering a readiness to take a hand in community affairs.

THE ANNUAL DINNER

The third Annual Dinner of The Neighborhood Garden Association was held at the Young Women's Christian Association.

More than two hundred people attended the dinner. The members of the Sponsoring Committees were seated at the tables with the Staff representatives from the Settlement Houses, and the Block Leaders on their Garden Blocks. This made possible a pleasant sharing of interests and enthusiasms.

Reports were given by each Garden Block Leader and by four Junior Members representing the Junior Garden Clubs.

Awards of Merit were presented to 18 first year Garden Blocks and to 31 Second Year blocks, the award being a Christmas Tree for the block at Christmas time.

Special Citations were awarded to

Mrs. Flora Davis, teacher at Alexander Wilson School
Mrs. Bertha Corbin, Staff Worker, St. Martha's Settlement
Mrs. Mattie Burton, Block Leader on 1500 Rodman Block
Mrs. Edna Ware, Block Leader on the 1300 S. 46th Block
Mrs. Catherine Winston, Block Leader on 1700 N. Beechwood Block

THE CHRISTMAS WORK SHOPS

Nearly four hundred people participated in the Christmas Workshops, and on many Garden Blocks every doorway had its swag of evergreens decorated with cones, or red berries or a gay, red bow.

On many blocks a Christmas Carol Service was held in which everyone, young and old participated.

On the 2000 Block on Pemberton Street a beautiful and deeply impressive service was held on the Sunday before Christmas to dedicate the star which had been placed above the street. The star was lighted at dusk, Christmas carols were sung, the story of the Wise Men was read from the Bible, and several brief Christmas messages were given. The service closed with a very beautiful solo, sung by one of the members on the block.

In 1957 The Neighborhood Garden Association completed its fifth year of endeavor. With the passing of each year it had become increasingly evident how many constructive and rewarding things had grown out of the Garden Block program. It is this factor which gave added impetus to the work.

The window boxes and flower bays and little gardens had not only brought into these neighborhoods beauty for the eye to enjoy and a new vision for the mind to contemplate, they had also been a torch to the spirit which had kindled in the hearts of the people a striving for a better way of life.

Before Memorial Day the planting of 7000 window boxes had been completed on 121 Garden Blocks. Of these, 58 were sponsored blocks and 63 were Independent Blocks which purchased their own plants at wholesale rates through The Neighborhood Garden Association.

PUBLICITY

The article about the work of the Association in the 1957 April issue of the Readers' Digest brought inquiries from Georgia, Missouri, Ohio, and many other sections of the country. Reprints of this article were made by Keep America Beautiful Inc. and were widely distributed, a copy being included in each package of introductory material sent out from the New York headquarters to towns and cities throughout the country. After a visit to Philadelphia to see the Garden Blocks the Executive Director wrote, "I had an opportunity to see your fine work in Philadelphia . . . and I am greatly impressed with the potentials for extending the Garden Block idea to every city in America."

In April the St. Louis Post-Dispatch asked one of its special correspondents to do a feature article on the work of The Neighborhood Garden Association which was published under the title, "Philadelphia's Miracle of the Flowers." To quote a few excerpts from the article,—". . . the deadly squalor of a slum area creates an apathy that goes to the marrow of its inhabitants—like the dry rot which sags the timbers of its homes. . . . The flowers proved a stimulus that caused a chain-reaction . . . a catalyst that sparked many other things,—good neighborliness, cleanliness, pride in homes and good citizenship. Flowers speak a universal language. They are not simply something to gaze upon. They are a way of life."

In May the National Association of Settlements met in Philadelphia and on Sunday afternoon, May 17th, a brief talk was given on the work of The Neighborhood Garden Association, the slides were shown, and a tour was taken of some of the garden blocks.

When the State Federation of Garden Clubs met in Philadelphia in September a model window box attractively planted and colored photographs of the Garden Blocks were on display in the rooms of the Pennsylvania Horticultural Society at the time of the opening tea.

Particularly heartening have been the many Garden Blocks which have begun to spring up spontaneously, from initiative within the block. These give promise of the eventual wide-spread acceptance of the Garden Block idea as a result of our pilot projects.

An interesting project was undertaken on one of our Garden Blocks. Unusually attractive flower boxes had been made by the men on the block and after their first Planting Day they were filled with pride and joy over the appearance of the block. However, on the block was a very large, trash-filled lot which had been of no particular concern to anyone, as it had been there for years. Two days after the boxes had been planted they called a general meeting of the people on the block. They decided that the lot should be cleared, and the suggestion was made that it be turned into a playground for the children, as there was no recreation area within walking distance. It was also decided to ask everyone on the block to do something to earn a little extra money to help pay for the fence and the play equipment which would be needed. Almost everyone on the block cooperated. One little girl of eleven, Wilhelmina Outlaw, made aprons and other fancy articles which she sold to people in the neighborhood and contributed ten dollars to the project. It did not take long to raise the money for the fence, and it was decided to build two long flower bays between the sidewalk and the fence. Before a month had passed the work had been completed and above the gate hung a sign, LATONA PLAYLAND.

"Beauty and blight are infectious.
Inoculate a neighborhood with either and it will spread."

A trash-filled lot made into Latona Playland

Magnolia tree in bloom

The Cheerful Garden Club creates a garden

ALEXANDER WILSON SCHOOL AREA

For several years the Cheerful Garden Club had been eager to secure permission to make a garden on the large vacant lot at the end of their street. Beyond the lot was a steep bank and below were the railway tracks. At last the permission was granted and work on the garden was begun. The students in the Landscape Design Course at the School of Horticulture in Ambler designed the garden. After the lot had been cleared it was leveled off and in the early spring a lovely magnolia tree and a flowering Japanese cherry tree were planted. A fence was erected on which climbing roses were planted. The flower beds were laid out, and a pleasant sitting area established. From mid-summer until late autumn the garden was gay and colorful and the members of the Cheerful Garden Club were justified in taking great pride in their accomplishment.

Climbing roses on the fence

A NEW AREA

It was inevitable that some of the areas in which the Association had developed Garden Blocks and vacant lot gardens would be affected by the Redevelopment Program of the city. This was the fate of Ken-Watt Court. The residents of the Court were relocated in various parts of the city, and they took the idea of window boxes and little gardens with them.

The following spring one member of the group who had been located at the Spring Garden Housing Project called the Chairman of the Association and asked her if she would come in and see if they could get some garden projects started there. A few days later she went in and they discussed the possibilities. When she found that Mrs. Carter had envisioned 1000 little door yard gardens she explained that the first year it would be wise to start just a few gardens and then to expand the program the following year. There were seven houses on each side of a large grass panel and they decided to do a little garden plot beside each doorway. A date was set for the planting and Mrs. Carter assured her that the plots would be prepared and ready.

It was an inter-racial group, Negro and Puerto Rican. On the day that the plants were brought in Mrs. Carter was distressed because one of the beds had not been prepared. She explained that the man was returning to Puerto Rico. By the end of the morning when the last little garden plot was being planted Mrs. Carter came rushing to the Chairman. "Look!" she said, as she pointed across to the Puerto Rican who was hard at work spading up his plot. "Have you any extra plants?"

Yes, there were extra plants and they took them over to him. "I no be here." he said. "They can have them."

He could not bring himself to go back to Puerto Rico and leave that little plot of ground unspaded and unprepared. And what a nice welcome it was for another Puerto Rican family who soon moved in.

Regal lilies in the border

WESTERN COMMUNITY AREA

During 1957 the "Green Thumb" Junior Gardeners were organized by Mrs. Elizabeth Forrester. The groups were organized on a block basis with a membership of boys and girls between the ages of 7 and 14. Upon initiation each member takes the pledge—"As a Green Thumb Junior Gardener, I promise to protect our flowers, birds and trees, and to help make and keep my home and our city beautiful."

There was an adult Block Counselor on each block who held regular meetings for the Junior Gardeners. Program Activities of Junior Gardeners were demonstrated twice monthly at Western Community House for Block Counselors and (revolving) Junior Gardeners representatives.

Under the skillful guidance of Mrs. Forrester a new interest came into the lives of these boys and girls. For them the high spots of the year were the trip to the Philadelphia Flower Show and the Annual Flower Show at Western Community House in which they eagerly participated, and the wonderful Christmas Workshop.

THE ANNUAL DINNER

Mrs. Edward L. Elliot and Mrs. George R. Haines, Co-Chairmen.

The fourth Annual Dinner was held at the Young Womens' Christian Association, on December 4th. Despite the unexpected blizzard one hundred and forty people were present. It was a deep regret that many others were prevented from attending.

The Annual Dinner is an event which holds much interest and inspiration for all groups, the Sponsoring Garden Clubs, the Settlement Houses, and the representatives from the Garden Blocks.

Citations were awarded to:

Western Community House; to Miss Margaret Coleman of Wharton Center, and to the following Garden Block Leaders

Mrs. Harriet Brown, 2000 Fernon Block
Mrs. Beatrice Hodges, 2000 Pemberton Block
Mrs. Lavinia McNeill, 2200 Carpenter Block
Mr. George Young, 1200 Rodman Street

The Halliday Family received the Family Award.

Reports were given by the Block Leaders on the award-winning blocks and by Junior representatives. Immediately following the report the slides were shown.

Sixteen blocks received Awards of Merit for one year of constructive effort. Twenty-seven blocks received Awards of Merit for two or more years of outstanding achievement.

THE CHRISTMAS WORKSHOPS

The Christmas Workshops have proved to be one of the most rewarding activities of the Neighborhood Garden Association as they have brought the festive spirit of the Christmas season into areas where there had been little expression before. Evergreen sprays gay with red bows and little bells, wreaths trimmed with small cones with bits of evergreens, small aluminum pie plates decorated with sprays of evergreens and red berries to be hung in the windows, and many other delightful and novel decorations were made by enthusiastic teen-agers and adults at the various workshops and a warm feeling of good fellowship prevailed everywhere.

Nine Christmas Workshops were held:

Calvary Settlement
Dixon House
Germantown Settlement
Our Neighbors Association
Richard Allen Homes
Saint Martha's Settlement
United Neighbors and Reed Street House
Western Community House
Wharton Center

The following remarks are quoted from reports given by the Settlement Staff Workers at the Autumn Meeting of The Neighborhood Garden Association in 1959:

"You can't do Garden Club work without doing community work. It fits in on all areas."

"The work is no longer on a block level. There is now interest on the neighborhood level. Neighbors who have a concern for other neighbors soon have a concern for the community."

"A child who has flowers interwoven into his character is a better, happier child."

"The Garden Blocks have brought a better way of life to the people in these areas."

"A child who builds a fence for a neighbor is going to have respect for property."

"There is involvement at all levels."

"It is a wonderful way to get people interested in their problems."

"It is a tool to neighborhood organization."

"It is a wonderful, natural way to get people to work together. One woman had lived on a block for 15 years and didn't even know the name of the person across the street."

"The influence on one block spreads into another."

"As leadership develops within a block there is increasing concern about neighborhood problems, such as gambling and its influence upon children."

"The program creates a sense of pride and develops better community relationships."

THE NEIGHBORHOOD GARDEN ASSOCIATION EXHIBIT IN THE PHILADELPHIA FLOWER SHOW

The Neighborhood Garden Association exhibit in the Philadelphia Flower Show in March, 1958, was a tremendous success. The exhibit was designed by Mrs. F. Joseph Stokes, Jr. We had a story to tell and with her marvelous creative ability she told it well.

In erecting the exhibit the members of her committee and some of the husbands worked with unflagging zeal. There was the façade of a shabby little brick house, uncared for and unloved, with a broken down chair and little piles of trash beside it. Next to it was the façade of a similar little brick house with freshly painted woodwork and flower boxes filled with the colorful bloom at its windows, and other plant materials skillfully used.

The contrast was so striking that almost everyone who passed along the aisle stopped for a few moments to look at the exhibit.

Enlarged photographs showing some of the Garden Blocks before they were planted and several weeks later were on display and aroused a great deal of interest in the work of the Association.

Members of the Neighborhood Garden Association Committee served as hostesses throughout the day and evening.

The exhibit received a well deserved Special Award of Merit.

A SYMPOSIUM

Later in the spring a symposium on the Past, Present and Future of The Neighborhood Garden Association was planned for the presidents of the Garden Clubs, the members of the sponsoring committees and other organizations associated with our program.

It offered to the members of these groups an opportunity to become more familiar with the work of The Neighborhood Garden Association. And it also offered an opportunity to share with each other ways they had found to be particularly effective in encouraging interest among their members, in planning their planting programs and in financing their projects. Many helpful and interesting suggestion grew out of these discussions.

Mrs. Edward L. Elliot acted as Moderator and Mrs. F. Joseph Stokes, Jr. presented the following report on the work of the Association.

"We, of the Executive Committee, on behalf of the Association and the citizens of Philadelphia with whom we have worked, wish to express our gratitude to you and the organizations which you represent for the wonderful contribution which you have made during the past six years. We have come a long way, comparatively fast, and these first years have proved the value of our Association.

"You have found the people with whom you work responsive and happier because of your contacts with them. You have been responsible for Community Centers reaching people who were apathetic and lonely. You have created in people an awareness of each other and a positive approach to what can be done in bettering themselves and their neighbors and their communities.

"In 1953 there were seven pilot Garden Blocks. We worked that year thru five Settlement Houses and the Richard Allen Homes, and there were 15 sponsoring Garden Clubs.

"In 1958 there are 159 Garden Blocks with approximately 15,000 window boxes and flower bays. And many vacant lots have become little gardens or play lots. There were eleven co-operating Settlement Houses and 37 Sponsoring Groups. This is amazing growth for only six years.

"Actually, we have expanded far beyond this, for the idea of Philadelphia's Garden Blocks has been carried to Boston, Detroit, Cleveland and other cities. Last March two people made a trip from St. Louis to obtain information about the work of The Neighborhood Garden Association and they have launched a similar project. In December two people flew down from the Buffalo area and are now organizing their program. And inquiries have been received from Savannah, Cinncinnati and Pittsburgh. The head of the American Farm School in Greece has taken the idea back with him and plans to use it in whole villages.

"Christmas Workshops have been organized to draw people together and show them how to carry beauty over into the winter months. Local Garden Clubs and Junior Garden Groups have been started, and a very popular Flower Show is held each autumn. Blocks are uniting for social get-togethers, for childrens' projects and for civic improvement. There have been six Annual Dinners, well attended, where citations have been presented to out-standing leaders and awards to blocks for fine achievements.

"We have confidence now, confidence that The Neighborhood Garden Association of Philadelphia is an organization which is needed, confident that people everywhere become intensely interestd in the idea and in the results which have been achieved.

"We have established a fine and solid foundation upon which to build the future."

A number of points of particular interest were developed during the discussions which followed. The importance of having a deep understanding of the problems of the people with whom we work was stressed. It is a long step from apathy to civic pride, and sometimes in the more depressed areas the progress seems slow, but with a wise and understanding approach much may be accomplished. Occasional disappointments are inevitable, but must be accepted with the realization that they serve to create a greater challenge.

One group spoke of its concern over the fact that one of the Garden Blocks with which its members had worked was to be demolished to make way for a housing development. It was pointed out to the group that their work had not been in vain, as it had been the experience of the Association that when people move from a Garden Block onto another block, or are relocated in a new area one of the first things they strive to do is to organize a window box or garden project. The fourteen Community Gardens which were so successful in the Spring Garden Housing Project were the result of the efforts of one of our Ken-Watt members who had been relocated there when Ken-Watt Court was demolished.

NEW PLAY AREAS ON GARDEN BLOCKS

A fine large playground was developed through the cooperative efforts of four Garden Blocks in South Philadelphia. Mrs. Kizzie Holley, the Block Leader on the 2000 Watkins Block, persuaded the Block Leaders on the nearby Fernon, Pierce and Opal Blocks to join with her in establishing a play ground on a large lot beside a Church in the area. She had obtained permission to use the lot, provided the neighbors would finance it and give the necessary supervision. Every month during the summer some event was given to raise money for the project: a Bazaar in August, a Rummage Sale in September, a Barbecue in October. The fence was put up in July, and tot-swings, junior-swings and the sand pit had been completed by October, the work being done by the men on the Garden Blocks. It was a fine example of community participation in a worthwhile project.

At the same time another group of women in North Philadelphia were making a Play lot on another vacant lot, under the direction of Mrs. Mattie Waters, the Garden Block Leader on the 1600 Stiles block. The following letter written to The Neighborhood Garden Association tells the story.

> The slides that were shown at Our Neighbor's Association meeting inspired the members of our block to undertake such an endeavor. As a result we received permission to clean out a vacant lot on our block and are now in the process of converting it into a playground for small children.
>
> All the neighbors pledged their whole-hearted support into making this a block project. The lot was cleared of all debris, and we will put sand in it to make it safe for the children. The men enclosed the area with a wooden fence which they erected on a Saturday. As a result of a successful chicken dinner we have enough money in our treasury to equip the playground. Needless to say, this is the first project of this sort ever attempted in this community.
>
> Out of gratitude we would like to invite you to see this playground, a project made successful by all our efforts.
>
> 1611 Stiles Street Block Club, Mattie Waters,
> President

On July 4th a beautiful dedication ceremony was held. Father Michelman pronounced a blessing upon the playground and a neighborhood picnic followed. From July 4th to the 30th of September a Bible Class was held in the playground every morning at 10 o'clock, followed by supervised play for the rest of the day.

Another letter of appreciation: from a new area.

On behalf of the members of the Civic Association of the 1100, 1200 and 1300 blocks on Rodman Street I wish to express deepest appreciation for the beautiful flowers you so unselfishly donated to us, to make our street a credit to the community which we live in.

Flowers are such an instrument in bringing people together. In planting these flowers it made you forget any problems that ordinarily would run across your mind.

George Young, Chairman
Louise Smith, Secretary

A sidewalk Garden

RICHARD ALLEN HOMES

A comprehensive and very successful program was undertaken at the Richard Allen Homes during the season of 1958. As a result of cooperative efforts of the Management, the residents and the Neighborhood Garden Association, several outstanding Demonstration areas were developed.

Early in the spring an outdoor meeting was held in each area, which provided an opportunity to discuss with the residents the garden program and other matters relevant to home improvement.

Mr. Berry, the Manager, and Mrs. Nichols, the Home Advisor, and their assistants also visited all the schools in the area. As a result of the talks given at the school assemblies many Junior Aids were enlisted. Adult Area Leaders were also appointed who were responsible for carrying on many of the details in connection with the program.

The plots in front of each house were prepared for planting and arrangements were made to secure low wire fencing as a protection for the plots. The flowers which were so generously brought in by the Garden Clubs and the 4-H Clubs were planted, and throughout the summer months the little gardens were gay with bloom, some of the plants continuing in flower until almost Thanksgiving time.

The Junior Aids swept and hosed down the areas and kept them free of litter, and also helped with the care of the gardens. As an expression of appreciation for their fine efforts each group had a party given in its honor at the end of the season.

As it is not possible for The Neighborhood Garden Association to work with all of the new Housing Projects in this area which have requested help, it is hoped that these well-organized Demonstration Garden Areas at the Richard Allen Homes will serve as a model upon which other Housing Developments can base their projects.

In presenting her report at the Autumn Meeting of The Neighborhood Garden Association Mrs. Nichols brought it to a close by saying: "I am a dreamer, and you've got to believe so firmly in your dreams that you finally persuade others to believe."

Among the pre-school children an imaginative garden club was organized called The Cookie Garden Club. As Mrs. Nichols put it—"They are too young to do good for goodness' sake and you have to give them something as a reward." The members of the Cookie Garden Club acted as a Garden Patrol which proudly protected the flowers at all times.

In the autumn all the Area Leaders and many other residents gathered in the auditorium for a Special Award Presentation Program. The program closed with several beautiful solos sung by a very talented member of the group.

More than 70 members participated in the Christmas Workshop sponsored by the Lansdowne Garden Club.

CONTINUING GROWTH

In the spring of 1959 forty-nine new Garden Blocks were planted, bringing the total number of blocks to 208. In order to better grasp the extent of these projects it is interesting to realize that if all the 208 Garden Blocks were consecutive blocks there would be 24 miles of Garden Blocks, gay with window boxes and flower bays and climbing roses.

"When one has a flower box at one's window or a plant on one's door-step it says 'I do care.' And it is often the first step towards caring—the first step towards neighbors learning to work together for community improvement."

This statement was made by one of our Garden Block Leaders in North Philadelphia, Mrs. Mary Newton, and expresses so eloquently one of the great, underlying strengths which has made the work of The Neighborhood Garden Association such a constructive force and so far-reaching in its influence. The flowers have been an extraordinarily effective means to an end, for they have touched the hearts of the people as nothing else could have done.

Garden Blocks are pleasant blocks upon which to live, they are happy places for children to be growing up, they are blocks where neighborliness and good will dwell, blocks where the residents not only have a feeling of dignity and pride but where they also acquire a growing awareness of their responsibilities as citizens in a wider community.

NEW AREAS

Early in January in the winter of 1959 the Mothers' Group at the McMichael School, located in the Mantua area in West Philadelphia, asked the Principal if an illustrated lecture could be given at their January Meeting about the work of the Neighborhood Garden Association in other parts of the city.

As a result of this lecture 3 pilot Garden Blocks were developed during the spring. The 3500 Block on Wallace Street was sponsored by the St. Andrews Church Committee and became one of our most outstanding blocks. The houses on one side of the street were on a raised terrace which made possible the development of a series of lovely little gardens. On the other side of the street the houses had porches and little fenced dooryards. The window boxes and porch boxes were filled with flowers, climbing roses were planted and a great many perennials were used in the gardens. Everyone on the block participated and it was a joy to drive through the block.

Another school in that general area became interested in the Garden Block program and an illustrated lecture was given at a special School Assembly to which parents were invited. Five Garden Blocks were developed, sponsored by the Social Service Club at Ambler Junior College (formerly the Pennsylvania School of Horticulture). On the 3700 block on Warren Street, a particularly drab block, the window boxes inspired the men on the block to paint not only the woodwork but in most cases the entire fronts of their homes.

Another interesting new project was undertaken as a result of a request from the Pennsylvania Society for the Protection of Children from Cruelty. After making a survey to see what could be done to make the rear courtyard less dreary, several very long flower boxes, supported by legs, were made by some country neighbors, and after they had been put in place against the brick wall at the rear of the yard and filled with good country soil, the Green Thumb Junior Gardeners from Western Community House planted the flowers. The plants received excellent care and over the years have brought a much appreciated beauty into this otherwise drab spot which has been sponsored by the Random Garden Club.

REPORTS FROM OTHER CITIES

Cities continue to send delegations to observe the work which is being done by The Neighborhood Garden Association in Philadelphia, and it is heartening to receive reports from areas where projects have been organized as a result of such visits. Boston sent a fine report of the excellent Garden Block program which was developed under the auspicies of the Federation of South End Settlements. The Tonawanda Project, near Buffalo, was successfully launched and a most interesting report was received telling of this endeavor.

LECTURES

Each year brings an increasing number of requests for lectures about the work of the Neighborhood Garden Association. Among the groups to which the lecture was presented in 1959 were the Rectory Club of the Diocese of Pennsylvania, the Men's Service Club of the Germantown Y.M.C.A., the Homemaking Consultants of the School District of Philadelphia, the Beacon Hill Branch of the Woman's National Farm and Garden Association, the Garden Club of Wilmington, to which representatives from twenty Federated Garden Clubs and the heads of all the Settlement Houses were invited.

THE COMMITTEE OF VOLUNTEERS

In recent years many blocks have applied to become Garden Blocks for which we have had no sponsoring group available. Contributions from many individuals and from organizations to which lectures have been given, are used to purchase flowers for these blocks, but it has sometimes been difficult to provide for the transportation of the plants and for the much needed assistance on Planting Day. In order to meet these needs the Executive Committee decided to organize a Committee of Volunteers. The members of this new Committee, which will be under the Chairmanship of Mrs. Newbold Ely, will be persons who may not be members of any garden club but who would be glad to give an occasional half day during May and early June to help with the planting of a Garden Block.

THE ANNUAL DINNER was held on November 18th and was an event of great significance. Mayor Dilworth was the guest of honor and among the distinguished guests at the head table were Mr. Robert W. Crawford, Commissioner of Recreation, Mr. Edmund N. Bacon, Executive Director of the City Planning Commission, Dr. Stephen B. Sweeney, Head of the Fels Institute of Local and State Government at the University of Pennsylvania, Mrs. Dorothy Montgomery, Director of the Philadelphia Housing Association, Mrs. Constance Dallas, member of the Commission on Human Relations, and Mrs. Ferdinand Fetter, well-known author.

In his address Mayor Dilworth expressed his appreciation of the work which has been accomplished through the co-operative efforts of the Settlement Houses, the Garden Clubs, Church groups, Schools, and the residents on the blocks. He emphasized particularly the contrast between the attractiveness and the cleanliness of the Garden Blocks which he had visited and other blocks in the vicinity which were strewn with litter. And he urged that the work of The Neighborhood Garden Association be carried on with increased zeal in order that Philadelphia might again have something of the aspect of William Penn's "Greene Countrie Towne.'

Citations for outstanding achievement were awarded to nine Garden Block Leaders, and seventy-seven Garden Blocks received Awards of Merit.

Reports were given by Representatives from the Settlements and the school areas. Brief excerpts from two of the reports are given below.

Several new blocks joined our group and each block had its portion of pride and beauty . . . Our Calvary Flower Club, under its leader, Miss

Cramer, has brought us together, and togetherness is like a chain. When a new link is added the chain grows stronger, so it is up to us, individually and collectively, to keep the chain growing.

We have excellent attendance at each meeting and when summer and outdoor gardening are far spent we turn our attention to planning Christmas baskets for those less fortunate than we are.

Oh! yes, the Calvary Flower Garden still has roses blooming (November 18th).

We pray good health and spiritual guidance on each of us until we meet again.

Mrs. Ruby Johnson
Representing Calvary Settlement Area

We join with all the other groups in repeating that with beauty in the block comes the gradual change—clean streets, paint and cheer, and better neighbors.

Mrs. Catherine Fox
Representing Reed Street Neighborhood House Area

Each year has brought new opportunities for service to The Neighborhood Garden Association, and its areas of endeavor and its influence have been constantly extended.

The year 1960 was one of unprecedented growth. A total of 64 new Garden Blocks were planted and the plant orders sent in by Independent Blocks totaled over $2,000.

The Garden Block program has proved such a unique and vital force in neighborhood conservation and has had such an impact upon the lives of the people on the blocks that it has received national and international recognition. A well-illustrated feature article about The Neighborhood Garden Association was recently published in a leading magazine in Holland, and requests for information about our Garden Block program have been received from Australia, India and Japan.

THE 4-H CLUBS

Each year the Neighborhood Garden Association had received an increasing number of requests to work with youth groups. The Executive

Committee, after careful consideration, decided that the organization of some urban 4-H Clubs might offer the best opportunities for city-wide participation.

The 4-H Clubs have always been rural clubs, but we felt that they would also have much to offer to city boys and girls. The clubs are under the direction of the Federal and State Extension Services and are recognized as one of the finest and most constructive organizations for youth in our country. The national membership totals over a million and a half, the boys and girls ranging from ten to twenty years of age. A few attempts had been made in other areas to form urban clubs, but with little success, due to the lack of local adult leaders.

We realized that on our 272 Garden Blocks we had some fine, potential 4-H Club Leaders, and that the many vacant lots on our Garden Blocks would provide excellent opportunities for 4-H Club garden projects.

After a great deal of discussion the Executive Committee decided to suggest to Mr. William White, the County Agent in Philadelphia, that The Neighborhood Garden Association would be glad to cooperate with the Agricultural Extension Service in organizing some pilot urban 4-H Clubs. This suggestion was enthusiastically received.

Mrs. Forrester, of Western Community House, consented to act as the Adult Leader of this first pilot group and the Oasis Green Thumb 4-H Club was organized. An excellent program was set up and the enthusiastic response of the members was most heartening. The sense of belonging to a fine organization with national scope offered a stimulating challenge. At the beginning of each meeting the boys and girls recite in unison their 4-H Club pledge.

I pledge my head to clearer thinking,
        my heart to greater loyalty,
        my hands to larger service and
        my health to better living
for my club, my community and my country.

Among the projects undertaken by this Pilot Club were the planting and storing of tulip and hyacinth bulbs for later bloom indoors, the growing of paper-white narcissus bulbs in bowls, the making of an identification chart of the foliage of trees, and the planting of a dish garden.

For its first community project the members of the Club decided to grow bowls of paper-white narcissus to take to sick children in the hospital. They also decided to plant an extra project each time for sick or elderly people.

Oasis Green Thumb 4-H Club—
planting border in City Hall

Four Leaf Clover 4-H Club

4-H Club Gardens

Crusader's 4-H Club

Tree Trunks 4-H Club,   Before   After

Site of Gardenia 4-H Club
and the garden one year later

OPERATION PLANT LIFT

A very interesting project was undertaken as the result of an illustrated talk on the work of The Neighborhood Garden Association, which was given to the Episcopal Young Churchmen at St. Thomas' Church in Whitemarsh.

It so happened that a few weeks later the Church of Saint Simon the Cyrenian in South Philadelphia asked if the Association could give them assistance in making a garden on a bare, unsightly lot between the new Parish House and the street. The Association was glad to grant the request. A design was drawn up for the garden, and as soon as the weather was favorable a Saturday work project was set up and the boys and girls of the city Parish were shown how to prepare the ground and make it ready for planting. A small flowering cherry tree, a crape myrtle and a few evergreen shrubs, purchased with a donation from the Young Churchmen, had been brought in and were planted according to the plan.

The rest of the story is beautifully told in an article by Mrs. Burquin Morrow of St. Thomas' Church, from which the following excerpt is quoted.

"As Rogation Sunday drew near, there were those in the Parish who thought again of this garden program, this time in the light of a sharing between city church and country church . . . As so often happens in the work of the church, the two needs were answered by each other—the need of St. Thomas' to do something of service . . . the need of St. Simon the Cyrenian for a helping hand. So was born 'Operation Plant Lift.'

"Flyers were distributed to adults at St. Thomas', as well as to the Church School children. The flyers listed the types of plants needed, and asked that they be brought to Church on Rogation Sunday. The plants were placed in the grove by the church and following the Family Service the plants were blessed by the Rector.

"On Sunday afternoon 22 boys and girls in working clothes, and carrying trowels, loaded three station wagons with plants and with their clergy and youth advisors they drove into the city to the Church of St. Simon the Cyrenian. Their co-workers from the city parish were waiting for them and they went to work. Marigolds, petunias, lantanas and geraniums were soon showing their colors in the flower borders and everyone felt a glow of accomplishment. Unfortunately a shower dampened the ardor of the group somewhat but nothing stopped the planting.

"When the last flowers had been planted the Rector called the group together for a short dedication service and blessed the garden and those whose work it was. The service was a far cry from the quiet of the country churchyard where the plants had been blessed, but the service carried its own strength, and all present were encompassed in one Divine fellowship. Then the trowels were rounded up, and a happy, united group made their way inside to spend a half hour in fellowship over coffee, punch and cookies.

"Fifteen hundred years ago, Rogation Sunday was the time of 'Beating the bounds', blessing each church's physical property lines and what they bounded. Could we hopefully suggest that we are now learning that the Church has no bounds except those of human limitations? . . . Can those Christians who are fortunate in being blessed with God's acreage look to Rogation Sunday as a time for stretching their hands in fellowship to those whose property bounds are marked by cement and asphalt, always recognizing that it is only as we forget imaginery boundaries and ask for God's blessing on corporate service in His name that we many expect the riches of every season to have Christian meaning for us all."

For many years the Episcopal Young Churchmen of St. Thomas' Church in Whitemarsh planted a Garden Block in North Philadelphia on Rogation Sunday.

OPERATION OUTREACH

In March 1960 an illustrated lecture on the work of The Neighborhood Garden Association was given to a very large group in Washington. The audience was composed of representatives from all the civic organizations, garden clubs and settlement houses in Metropolitan Washington. Following the lecture many requests were received for the duplicate set of slides and several projects were started.

A very successful program was carried through at the Northwest Settlement House. Excerpts from the following letters tell the story of this project very eloquently.

I cannot help but personally express my thanks to you for having shown us both the goal and the way to reach that goal in our under-privileged areas. So many people think of Washington as their capital of white marble columns and enduring stone structures. They never see the slums, nor hear of the very low income people who dwell in the small tenements. For these, who are God's children, even as you and I, you have made flowers bloom. Thank you for helping us see how we can try to follow in your foot-steps.

Rosaline Fisher

April 5, 1960   President of Northwest Settlement House

June 24, 1960
Washington, D.C.

I am not surprised to report to you that hard work and a sincere approach to the people on the blocks in our area about the Window Box project have paid off in wonderful dividends—both in the discovery of new and unknown leadership, and in the enjoyment of working together for Neighborhood improvement.

Eight blocks have been organized and most of these are having weekly meetings. Planting Day on May 21st was a tremendous experience, 102 families being involved. Several community groups were asked to participate. The school woodwork shops made the boxes, a Civic association and the Inter-Church Committee on Urban Renewal helped the Garden Club in providing the flowers.

We are looking forward to judging days in July and a public meeting of all blocks in September. The Block Leaders have had a Television appearance and will talk on Radio next week.

We thank you for introducing us to such a wonderful citizen project. We have had many more adults in our program than ever before, as a result of this project.

Very gratefully yours,
Grace S. Lormans, Director
Northwest Settlement House

LECTURES

During 1960 twenty-four lectures on the work of The Neighborhood Garden Association were given to such widely varied groups as the Four Rivers' Garden Club in Annapolis, the Department of Landscape Architecture at the University of Pennsylvania, the Raymond Rosen Housing Project in North Philadelphia, the Scranton Womens' Club, the Board of Directors of the Agricultural Extension Service, and the Womens' Democratic Club of Philadelphia.

As a result of these talks Garden Blocks have been developed in several new areas, and a most successful garden project was launched at the Raymond Rosen Homes.

THE COMMITTEE OF VOLUNTEERS

Under the able chairmanship of Mrs. Newbold Ely the Committee of Volunteers carried through a superbly organized program. There were 18 members on this new committee and they gave most generously of their time and skills. Twenty-nine Garden Blocks were planted by the committee. This alone was a significant accomplishment, but the work of the Committee of Volunteers did not end when the planting season was ended, as is evident in the following excerpt from the Chairman's report presented at the Autumn Meeting of the Association.

"Members of our committee revisited our blocks several times during the summer, as well as many other blocks—showing interest and concern and appreciation of good effort, and often explaining again the care of the boxes which, although it seemed simple to us, is not always simple for people who have had no previous experience with flowers.

"This continuation of the friendly relation started on Planting Day led to many delightful experiences, such as attending a Bible Class one morning which was held on a tot-lot on one of our Garden Blocks by a remarkable block leader who has held this class for two weeks each summer for many years. Although she works at night she manages to teach, keep busy and inspire over 80 boys and girls for the entire morning. This visit lead to a picnic for the Bible Class, given by one of the Volunteers with the help of other members of the committee. Two bus loads of children and mothers, totaling about 125 people arrived, singing and eager. The mothers relaxed in the shade while the children, many of whom had never seen the country, sampled the joys of woods, fields, wild flowers, a stream to wade in and trees to climb.

"At the picnic we learned of a newly cleared vacant lot on one of our new blocks which was badly in need of a fence to keep it from reverting to its former state. One of the Volunteers had just taken down a high picket fence and within a week it was delivered and immediately put up by the combined efforts of the entire block. A large slide, outgrown by grandchildren, was sent in at the same time. Several other pieces of playground equipment were also located by volunteers and sent to another tot-lot.

"In visiting another block it was discovered that a rubbish-filled, rat-infested old garage had been cleaned and repaired by neighborhood boys for a club house, the name of the club being the Acorn Club. But they had nothing to sit on and no money for games or equipment. The Volunteers located benches, a book case, books for all ages, a garden table, crayons, coloring books and games. The club came alive. An opening Block Party was held with dancing in the street, refreshments and fun for all.

"I know that I speak for all the volunteers when I repeat what we have said so frequently to each other—'Nothing could have been more rewarding or more fun!'"

ALEXANDER WILSON SCHOOL PROJECT

Great preparations were made in the spring of 1960 for Planting Day as a new type of program was launched. The children left for school that bright May morning with eagerness, as the oldest child in the family was carrying an empty shoe box in which to bring home the flowers for the family window box.

The plants from the sponsoring schools in the suburbs began to arrive shortly after nine o'clock, some in station wagons, some in school buses bringing not only plants but also boys and girls and teachers who wanted to see the project in action.

After the plants were unloaded and sorted into window box combinations the children came down, class by class with their teacher. The oldest child in the family brought the empty shoe box into which were put the flowers for the family window box—a bright geranium, some gay petunias and perhaps a verbena or a lantana. By the time the noon bell sounded the plants had all been distributed and hundreds of happy children went home for lunch, the head of the family carrying the flowers with great care and pride.

It is indeed gratifying to see how the love of flowers spread through this entire community as a result of the project at the school. As one teacher wrote, "It lifts the heart just to walk about and see the garden plots, many of which were once filled with weeds and rubbish, now beautiful with flowers. One man has even built a patio beside his porch so his wife can enjoy their garden more. You will never know what life and joy you have brought into this neighborhood!"

Boys and girls from private schools bring flowers to the Alexander Wilson school

Children with flowers for their window boxes to take home

RAYMOND ROSEN HOMES

As an outgrowth of the talk given to a group of women a Garden Club was formed which was destined to have a tremendous influence on many of the residents at the Raymond Rosen Homes. Under the skilled guidance of Mrs. Emma Collins, the Home Advisor, a remarkably fine program was carried out. This new venture received the encouraging support of Mr. Beckett, the Manager and also of the Maintenance Department. Top soil and peat moss were supplied, grass seed was furnished and garden tools were made available for use.

With this support the enthusiastic members of the Raymond Rosen Garden Club went to work. They held bake sales to raise money to buy plants and small shrubs. They prepared their garden beds with care, they used their childrens' little wagons to haul rocks from a vacant lot to make little rock gardens.

In May the members of the Garden Club gathered to watch the planting of a small Demonstration Garden in front of the Administration Building by the Chairman of The Neighborhood Garden Association. Each step was explained and the requirements of the various plants were discussed. The planting was followed by a question and answer period.

In the autumn a small flower show was held and the gardens were judged by members of The Neighborhood Garden Association.

VISIT TO THE FLOWER SHOW

Among the high lights of the year was the visit to the Philadelphia Flower Show, as the Officials of the Show again graciously extended this privilege to residents on Garden Blocks when accompanied by a Staff Worker with a letter granting this permission.

A SEAL FOR THE ASSOCIATION

The Executive Committee decided that the Neighborhood Garden Association should have an attractive seal and Mrs. Charles Platt, a member of the Board of Directors, and a very gifted artist, was asked if she would be willing to design it. She was happy to do this for the Association and everyone was delighted with the design which had great distinction.

It was decided that in the future, on Planting Day, a seal would be given to each participant on the block to put in her window. Seals were also provided for all participants on the Independent Garden Blocks. The seal is shown on the opposite page.

RE-ORGANIZATION

In order to strengthen its rapidly expanding program and meet the increasing demands for its services The Neighborhood Garden Association, after careful consideration, decided to reorganize the structure of its governing body. In the spring of 1961 a new set of By-laws was adopted and the former Neighborhood Garden Association Committee was superseded by a Board of Directors.

For nine years the work of the Association had been conducted entirely on a volunteer basis, but with our rapidly expanding program the load had become increasingly heavy for those handling the administrative details, and the Board of Directors realized that it was imperative for the Association to have professional assistance.

A grant from one of the Foundations made it possible for The Neighborhood Garden Association to achieve this goal. At the Annual Dinner the announcement was made that Mrs. Elizabeth Forrester had been appointed Executive Director of the Association. Mrs. Forrester had been closely associated with the work of the Association from its beginning and for six years had served as Secretary of the Executive Committee. In 1954, while Program Director at Western Community House, Mrs. Forrester organized the Oasis Garden Club and later, as Executive Director at Western Community House, more than 50 Garden Blocks were organized under her direction. The Board of Directors felt that with her background and experience and her creative ability Mrs. Forrester would have an opportunity to open many new vistas for the Association in the years which lay ahead.

WELCOME TO SPRING PROGRAM

The Block Leaders on our Independent Garden Blocks were invited to attend a special program on the first day of spring, March 21st.

Plans for spring work were discussed, new window box charts and the new seals were given out and order blanks for plants were distributed. Mr. White, of the Extension Service, gave a talk on the National 4-H Clubs and slides were shown by Mrs. Bush-Brown highlighting the use of flowers in European cities. Refreshments were served by the Committee of Volunteers and each of the two hundred Garden Block Leaders was presented with a lovely, small coleus plant, donated by the Volunteers. It was an evening of good fellowship enjoyed by everyone.

THE 4-H CLUBS

The incredible success of the 4-H Club garden projects on vacant lots in widely scattered sections of the city, and the eagerness and enthusiasm of the members are convincing evidence of the tremendous potentials of urban 4-H Clubs.

Our pilot 4-H Club, the Oasis Green Thumb 4-H Club, was organized in November 1960 and proved so successful that 14 additional clubs were organized during 1961 with a total membership of 202 boys and girls, ranging in age from 10 to 19 years. The names selected for the various clubs were very interesting.

Berean Center 4-H Club	Oasis Green Thumb 4-H Club
Better Citizens 4-H Club	Pioneer 4-H Club
Busy Bee 4-H Club	Planters 4-H Club
Community Builders 4-H Club	Richard Allen Homes 4-H Club
Four Leaf Clover 4-H Club	Roots and Stems 4-H Club
Happy Flowers 4-H Club	Uberville Junior 4-H Club
Ivy 4-H Club	Uberville Senior 4-H Club
Youthful Gardeners 4-H Club	

The first Adult Leaders' Workshop was held on April 27th. These Workshops were held one evening a month throughout the year, and were of inestimable value to our fine group of Adult Leaders. At these meetings the program for the coming month was discussed, demonstrations on such things as seed sowing, the making of cuttings, potting up bulbs and planting dish gardens were given and special events were planned.

The project undertaken by all the clubs in the spring and early summer was Unit I in the 4-H "Plan and Plant for Beauty Series," being a garden of annual flowers, starting with young plants. Each club garden was planned as a whole and every member had his or her own section to plant and care for. Through the generous efforts of the 4-H Committee, of which Mrs. Newbold Ely was chairman, fencing and top soil were supplied and more than 7,500 young plants were brought in for the 4-H gardens.

The pilot Oasis Green Thumb 4-H Club undertook as a Community Project the planting and maintenance of a 150 foot flower border in City Hall Court Yard for which it received a Special Citation from the Mayor. Each member of the club had a ten foot section to plant and care for.

In September all the individual gardens were judged, and on Achievement Night, which is a very important event in the life of any 4-H Club boy or girl, certificates were presented for the completion of the project, and blue, red and white ribbons were awarded. The exceptionally high number of blue ribbons testified to the excellent care which these 4-H gardens received throughout the season.

In August a 4-H "round-up" was held, being a bus trip which made it possible for the members to visit each other's gardens, and enjoy a jolly picnic lunch together. A prize essay contest was also conducted and awards were made at the Annual Dinner.

In the autumn the Pilot Club undertook the House Plant Project, the Uberville Senior Club, the Electricity Project and the Junior Clubs the Indoor Bulbs and Dish Garden Projects.

Members of the Pilot Club took orders for dish gardens for Christmas and were very successful in this initial venture. Other clubs planned to do the same in their neighborhoods.

Christmas Workshops were held by all the clubs. The Committee of Volunteers brought in the greens and taught the members how to make lovely swags and wreaths and other festive decorations.

The 4-H Clubs were most grateful to the 4-H Committee and the Committee of Volunteers and their Adult Leaders for the wonderful help which was given them in getting their projects off the launching pad the first year.

THE COMMITTEE OF VOLUNTEERS

Under the Chairmanship of Mrs. Newbold Ely, the Committee of Volunteers carried on its work with dedication and zeal. The Committee took entire charge of the plant orders received from Independent Blocks, which was a tremendous undertaking, as it involved the tabulation and placing of the orders and the delivery of 5,500 plants to the various blocks and 4-H Club gardens.

Members of the Committee served as judges for the Flower Show at the Richard Allen Homes and for the area gardens at the Raymond Rosen Housing Project. They worked untiringly throughout the summer, helping with the preparation and planting of the 4-H Club gardens, and in the autumn they gave the 4-H Club Leaders a glorious day in the country.

RAYMOND ROSEN HOUSING PROJECT

At an early spring meeting of the Raymond Rosen Home and Garden Club it was decided to engage in an all-out area competition, thus bringing into use the knowledge and experience gained during the previous year. An announcement was made that a Silver Challenge Cup would be awarded in the autumn by The Neighborhood Garden Association to the area which had been judged the most outstanding.

Several very successful plant sales were held, the flowers being delivered by the Committee of Volunteers. As the season advanced the enthusiasm increased and a tremendous effort was put forth to create dooryard gardens of distinction and beauty.

An excellent Flower Show was held in the autumn and the Challenge Cup was awarded to the winning area. Other awards were also made and several members of the Philadelphia Housing Authority made brief talks.

The Better Citizens 4-H Club was organized in May and it soon had a waiting list of nearly 100 boys and girls. By late summer additional leaders had been trained and the club had tripled its membership.

At the close of the season the following letter was received with a check enclosed from the Raymond Rosen Garden Club.

Dear Friends:

Thanks many times for bringing in the plants for our Sales. We had a grand time selling them to our residents. Even the children came to buy and ask instructions as to their care. It looks as though we are encouraging the gardeners of tomorrow.

Please accept this token of our love and appreciation to help some other group get started. The fine work you are doing and the joy and satisfaction you bring to many, giving them hour after hour of cheer and beauty can't be compensated in dollars and cents, but we remember the friendly out-stretched hand, the friendly smile, the patient instructions, and all the many sacrifices made by the members of your group.

These are the things we remember which prompt us to want to add our small bit toward the furtherance of a wonderful work so well done.

Thanks again, we are sincerely grateful our paths met.

Yours truly
Raymond Rosen Home and Garden Club

RICHARD ALLEN HOMES

There were 826 dooryard gardens at the Richard Allen Homes last spring. In October a very impressive ceremony was held in the auditorium and 138 Certificates of Merit were awarded to residents by the Philadelphia Housing Authority in recognition of the exceptional beauty and high standard of maintenance of their gardens. Fifteen members of the Golden Age Club also received Certificates of Merit for their window plants.

EXCERPTS FROM REPORTS

CALVARY SETTLEMENT. "There are 16 blocks in our group at Calvary with three more coming in next year. The flowers were very pretty; our streets were clean and well kept. The Dream Garden was just beautiful with an abundance of roses and other flowers. We take great pride in our activities at Calvary, always mindful of our fellow man, always trying to impart some of the joy and beauty that the Garden Club has brought into our lives, into the lives of others less fortunate . . . There are not words enough to express our gratitude to The Neighborhood Garden Association and Miss Frances Cramer, our Directress at Calvary Settlement House, for the sheer joy of living that they have brought into our Neighborhood and into our lives."

Mrs. Agnes Erland, President
Calvary Flower Club

LUTHERAN SETTLEMENT. "The following story is well worth relating to you and your Association, because it is typical of the worth of your work, and the gratifying results that come from the window boxes. The 3900 block of Mount Vernon Street is a small one, thirteen houses. There are seven two story row houses and six homes with porches and small front yards. Today the Mount Vernon Block has accomplished these impressive Neighborhood Improvements:
1. Each home and yard is beautifully decorated with window boxes or dooryard gardens.
2. The street is cleaned daily.
3. Back alleys are passable and free of debris.
4. Block nuisances are at a minimum.
5. The entire block has been painted from top to bottom.

A gardener with ten green fingers

"The interest in these other projects began on the day the flowers were planted. The residents did not approach landlords for help. They did these improvements on their own. They are proud of their block and themselves. They are thankful for The Neighborhood Garden Association's interest and contribution to their block improvement program."

BEREAN CENTER. "I began talking with Mrs. A. last winter. Early in February she called a meeting of the people on her block. There was a 100% response to the idea of having window boxes. The men on the block got together and helped paint each other's houses. A Boys' Club at the Center made the boxes. They even whitewashed the fences on the street. A couple of boys hauled enough bricks from a demolition project to build bays for roses.

"We added a new block a few weeks ago. That was a real victory. It had been hard to get into the block, but now the doors are open wide. We have a one-legged almost blind man who spends all his time sitting at his window. It is a pleasure to see his enjoyment of flowers. And there is a crippled woman who said it seems as if something new had come into her life when the flowers came on her street."

EACH YEAR PRESENTS A NEW CHALLENGE

The year 1962 was one of heartening growth. Sixty-one Garden Blocks were planted by the sponsoring Garden Clubs and the Committee of Volunteers. Nineteen of the blocks were in North Philadelphia, fourteen in South Philadelphia and twenty-eight in West Philadelphia.

THE HOME AND GARDEN CLUB at the Raymond Rosen Homes had a very active and successful year. In the autumn a beautiful program was given in the auditorium, combining a very fine Flower Show, the presentation of Awards and a delightful musical program.

The silver challenge cup, given by The Neighborhood Garden Association, is presented each year to the area which shows the greatest improvement. This stimulates a great deal of friendly rivalry among the twenty areas in the Housing Project, and it is considered a great honor to win the cup.

RITTENHOUSE SQUARE FLOWER MARKET. In 1962 the Neighborhood Garden Association was one of the beneficiaries of the Rittenhouse Square Flower Market. Under the able Chairmanship of Mrs. Sidney P. Clark, with Mrs. Edward T. Stuart as Vice-Chairman, the Association booth at the Flower Market was a great success. Pomandas, dish gardens and lovely flower arrangements were very popular items. It was a gala day for the members of the Board of Directors, and members of the sponsoring Garden Clubs and other volunteers who worked so enthusiastically together.

THE MANTUA AREA. The decision to undertake a long term, comprehensive project in the Mantua Area was reached after a conference with Mr. Edmund Bacon, Executive Director of the City Planning Commission, and Mr. Leo Molinaro, Executive Director of the West Philadelphia Development Corporation. The Mantua area is adjacent to the proposed University City.

COMMITTEE OF VOLUNTEERS. Under the very stimulating Chairmanship of Mrs. Newbold Ely, the committee took charge of the delivery of plants ordered by the Independent Blocks, and planted 26 Garden Blocks for which there were no sponsoring clubs. The Committee also helped with planting and judging the 4-H project gardens and assisted with the Rittenhouse Square Flower Market and the Christmas Workshops.

THE 4-H PROGRAM. During 1962 eleven new 4-H Clubs were organized, making a total of 26 clubs with a membership of 289 boys and girls between the ages of 10 and 19.

In March the new 4-H Neighborhood Improvement Program was launched. This was co-sponsored by The Neighborhood Garden Association and the Agricultural Extension Service of Pennsylvania State University, under a grant of the Sears-Roebuck Foundation. It was the first program of its kind in this country and may well become a pattern for clubs to follow in other urban areas.

Each club was asked to consider the needs of its community and to decide what project it would like to undertake for its improvement. Upon a given date the following details were to be submitted to the 4-H Neighborhood Improvement Committee: a brief narrative concerning the project, a sketch plan drawn to scale, if a vacant lot garden was considered, and a list of materials which would be needed. Suggestions for changes and improvements were made by the Committee when advisable. After full approval was given the Club received as a grant, the materials required for carrying out the plan—fencing, lumber, cement blocks, top soil and plants.

This program was a tremendous stimulus to 4-H Club Leaders and to Club Members as it made them aware of the needs of their community and presented them with a challenge. The results were beyond all expectations. Under the skillful and dynamic guidance of Mrs. William Harcum, Chairman of the 4-H Committee, miracles were performed. Trash-filled vacant lots became gardens of beauty and distinctive charm and were so well cared for that the flowers remained in bloom until late in the autumn.

In June two Senior 4-H Club boys were selected to attend a 4-H conference at Pennsylvania State University and in August three Senior girls, accompanied by Mrs. Forrester, attended the 4-H contests at the University, competing in the class for Flower Identification. It was a wonderful experience for both groups. Three of our fine Adult 4-H Leaders also had an opportunity to attend a Leader Conference on Youth Problems.

Three monthly workshops for Adult 4-H Leaders were held under the skilled direction of Mrs. Forrester, one in North Philadelphia, one in South Philadelphia and one in West Philadelphia.

WELCOME TO SPRING PROGRAM for the Leaders of our Independent Blocks was held March 21st at Strawberry Mansion Center. Plans for spring work were discussed, slides of some Garden Blocks and 4-H Gardens were shown, refreshments were served by the Committee of Volunteers and each guest received a coleus plant to take home. It was an evening of happy fellowship.

LECTURES. More than 40 requests for lectures were received in 1962. Lectures were given to audiences at the Brooklyn Botanic Garden, Nantucket Garden Club, University of Missouri, Rutgers University and Pennsylvania State University, and in many other areas.

In April a lecture was given at the National 4-H Club Conference in Washington, attended by delegates from 50 states, Puerto Rico and Canada.

Following this conference there was such a demand for the lecture that Sears-Roebuck Foundation offered to have duplicate sets of slides made with an accompanying tape recording and to make them available to every State Extension office. These sets and recordings were made by the Radio and Television Section of the Cooperative Extension Service at Pennsylvania State University.

MEMBERSHIP DRIVE. As it was becoming increasingly evident that it was of vital importance for The Neighborhood Garden Association to have an adequate annual income in order to continue its rapidly expanding program, this subject was brought up for discussion at the February 1963 meeting of the Board of Directors.

After thoughtful consideration it was decided to launch a drive for contributions. A Fund Raising Committee was appointed and under the Chairmanship of Mr. Alexander Hemphill plans for the drive were formulated.

A general appeal for Annual Membership was sent out. Three members of the Board of Directors graciously invited groups of friends to a Sunday afternoon reception at their homes. Upon these occasions a brief talk on the work of The Neighborhood Garden Association was presented and an appeal for contributions was made. Response to the appeal was heartening.

THE DEMONSTRATION GARDEN

In the early spring of 1963 The Neighborhood Garden Association, in cooperation with the Extension Service, began the development of a Demonstration Garden located at the corner of North 38th Street and Mt. Vernon Street in the Mantua area of West Philadelphia.

For several years the Association had hoped to find a favorable location for such a project and this site was ideal in many ways. It was ample in size and was readily accessible by public transportation from all parts of the city.

The lot had been vacant for many years and had accumulated most of the large scale junk in the area, such as junked cars, old bathtubs and refrigerators and various kinds of trash. Therefore the first concern was to have the lot cleaned off.

After this had been done work began on the plan for the garden. Many conferences took place with the Landscape Architect and general guide-lines were established.

It was agreed that the garden should be a Teaching Garden where people from all parts of the city and from surrounding areas could come and obtain information on garden problems and could see gardens of many types which were suited to city conditions. We all felt that in developing a series of small gardens very simple materials should be used which would be readily available. It was our hope that anyone visiting the garden would gather new ideas which he could adapt to his own home surroundings.

When the general plan was completed and approved it provided space for three model frontyard gardens, three model backyard gardens, a shrub garden, a perennial garden, a rose garden, a small herb garden, a vacant lot garden, a patio, a garden in-a-box, an identification garden. The plan also included two long flower borders beside the central path leading to the charming little Garden House. On the upper level a play area for children was to be developed.

The West side of the garden, which was planned by the Extension Service, included areas for many 4-H Club projects such as the Plan and Plant for Beauty Project, the Landscape Design Project, the Cut Flower Project, the Turf Project and the Vegetable Project.

It seemed an Herculean task to carry out the plan as the ground consisted of hard-packed cinders. There wasn't a fraction of an inch of soil on the entire area. This meant that after the ground had been leveled an enormous quantity of top soil would have to be brought in. It also meant that all the areas to be used for the various gardens would have to be on a higher level than the gravel paths. After considering various possibilities, it was decided that railway ties would be the best solution, and a freight carload of ties was ordered. For the next six weeks the trucks and the bulldozer took over, and the precious spring days slipped by.

At last the fence was completed, the last railway tie laid in place and the last piece of big equipment removed. It was the 25th of June.

Fortunately, the plants for the two long flower borders leading to the Garden House had been grown in wooden plant bands and were in good condition when they were brought in from the country in spite of the long delay. Many of them were just coming into bloom so within a few weeks the flower borders were colorful and gay.

It had been decided that the Garden Clubs which had sponsored the Garden Blocks over the ten year period from 1953 to 1963 should have the much desired privilege of designing and developing the various small gardens indicated on the plan. One exception was made for the newly formed local Mantua Garden Club.

Everyone was eager to begin work on these special gardens and for the next month and for the balance of the summer there was a great deal of activity in the Demonstration Garden.

The model Vacant Lot Garden was the first one to be planted. It was on a plot with a frontage of sixteen feet and a depth of thirty feet which are the exact measurements of the many vacant lots in the area where a house has been condemned and demolished. The aim was to show what could be accomplished through community effort in transforming a trash-filled lot into an attractive garden.

There is a central grass panel with a narrow path on each side leading to a pleasant sitting area at the rear. The paths are bordered with a three-foot bed of flowers, planned to give abundant bloom throughout the season.

The three model frontyard gardens varied in size. The first one of the group was attractively designed with a curving brick path to the door which was bordered with coral bells and other flowers. In one corner there is a bird bath on a pedestal, sheltered by a planting of carefully selected shrubs, and along the front there is a low, evergreen hedge. (Twin Valleys Garden Club)

In the next garden a very simple fence made of split, round, natural wood pickets has been used and there is a wooden arbor supporting a vine over the doorway. A brown brick path leads to the door and along the wall there is a pleached pyrocantha shrub bearing white flowers in spring and bright orange berries in the autumn. In a corner of the garden there is a Golden Chain tree (Laburnum vulgare) which bears lovely yellow panicles of bloom in the spring. In the garden beds bordering the path there is a charming planting of flowers in soft tones—white iris, bleeding heart, dusty miller, with an under-planting of vinca minor and spring bulbs. (Bala-Cynwyd Garden Club)

The third front yard garden, which is the smallest in size, shows what can be done on a very small plot. In a corner of the garden is a Golden Chain tree. In the center there is a half oval of grass with a path around it leading to the front step. The path is bordered with flowers: petunias, snapdragons, sweet alyssum and other annuals. Along the front of the garden there is a large green santolina at one end and a large grey santolina at the other end used as accents. (Mantua Garden Club)

These small frontyard gardens offer many practical and delightful suggestions for creating a bit of beauty along city streets.

The three backyard gardens also offer some imaginative ideas. One of the gardens was especially planned for a family with children and a dog, which necessitated putting most of the planting on a raised level where it would be protected from harm. This has been done very skillfully by using railway ties to hold the soil in place. Flowers, shrubs and a dogwood tree were planted on this upper level. A lower bed was protected by a pull-out, snap-in gate, such as is often used to protect very young children from falling down stairs. (The Gardeners)

Another backyard garden features a seat against a background of shrubs and a bird feeder. In one corner an evergreen vine (Euonymus radicans) was planted. This is being trained onto a wire frame surrounding a tall pole. If carefully pruned this will, in time, resemble a conical evergreen tree. The flower beds along the brick path leading to the seat are planted with a variety of flowers and spring bulbs. (Four Counties Garden Club)

The third backyard garden features plants which will grow well in dense shade and in partial shade. Many small city backyards have little, if any, sunlight and consequently little effort is made to have any bloom. This garden demonstrates that there are some flowers and many foliage plants, which will do well in shady locations such as: impatiens, which thrives extremely well in shade and will bloom throughout the season, wax begonias, fuchsias, torenia which is a dainty thing for the front of a border, and lobelia. Among foliage plants are the many new and very beautiful varieties of coleus and caladiums. All of these were included in the planting of the Shady Back Yard Garden.

THE PERENNIAL GARDEN includes many perennials which are well adapted to city conditions: coral bells, lythrum superbum, hardy candytuft, day lilies, shasta daisies, veronica, iris, phlox, blue flax (linum perenne) and columbines. The curved paths and the lovely planting of the large flowered clematis on the fence at the rear, add greatly to the charm of this garden. (The Weeders Garden Club)

THE SHRUB GARDEN displays a planting of well chosen shrubs, lilacs

The site

Rose garden, garden house and flower borders

The Demonstration Garden

A garden in a box

Door yard gardens

in the rear with hardy azaleas and other shrubs in the foreground, with an under-planting of English ivy and spring bulbs. (The Planters Garden Club)

THE ROSE GARDEN contains many lovely varieties of roses. If one has a place for just one rose in a small dooryard one can select *the* rose or, if space permits, a wider selection can be made. In a corner of the garden at the rear a star magnolia tree was planted which is the first thing to bloom with an early welcome to the Spring. (Huntingdon Valley Garden Club)

The small *HERB GARDEN* was planted with enticingly pungent herbs: lemon verbena, sage, rosemary and many other kinds. (The Philadelphia Unit of the American Herb Society)

The flower boxes along the front and sides of the Garden House were planted with pink geraniums, petunias, browallias and vinca minor. (Providence Garden Club)

A GARDEN IN A BOX. This box measuring 4 ft. by 4 ft., was designed especially for the city dweller with a small, paved back yard, and attracted much attention. It was planted with eight varieties of annual plants, in order to maintain continuous bloom from early spring until late autumn: petunias, sweet alyssum, snapdragons, Boston yellow daisy, verbenas, dwarf nicotiana, and blue sage and dwarf marigolds.

In the *IDENTIFICATION GARDEN* one finds a well-labeled plant of each type of flower found in the garden. If a visitor comes upon a flower which he is unable to identify he can go to the Identification Garden. It is like looking up something in the dictionary.

By late summer most of the planting in the Demonstration Garden had been completed with the exception of the trees and some of the shrubs which would be planted at a later time when they were dormant.

Visitors soon began to come. Among them was the local mailman, known affectionately by the neighbors as Mr. Mike. He came in every day as he went on his rounds and always had a pleasant greeting for those who were at work in the garden. One day he paused for a few moments to take a look down the long flower borders leading to the Garden House. The Chairman of The Neighborhood Garden Association happened to be standing near by and turning to her he remarked, "What music does for the ears, flowers do for the eyes, don't they?"

On another day a truck going past the garden stoped suddenly. The driver got out and came hurriedly into the garden. "What kind of a fence is that?" he asked, pointing to an English type hurdle fence. "Is it expensive?" He was assured that it was not expensive, when compared with the cost of other types, and that it was very easy to install. "We have a vacant lot on my block" he said before he left. "Could I bring some of the people on my block to see this?" He was assured that they would be welcome, and as a result of his brief visit a vacant lot on his block became a garden, in a far distant part of the city.

In the early spring of 1964 the planting in the Demonstration Garden was completed. Flowering cherry and flowering crab trees were planted at the intersection of the two major paths, and additional planting was done in some of the small garden areas.

WINDOW BOXES ON PARADE attracted a great deal of attention as they featured a wide variety of plants suited to different locations. For shady areas wax begonias, fuchsias, coleus, torenia and ivy were used in various combinations.

For sunny exposures geraniums, petunias, lantanas, dwarf marigolds, verbenas, dwarf zinnias and variegated vinca vine were used. There was one box gay with colorful portulacas which had been grown from seed sown directly in the window box, and another box in which dwarf nasturtiums had been sown.

Before the end of the season more than two thousand people had visited the Demonstration Garden. They came from every section of the city, from the suburbs, and from more distant points: Baltimore, Boston, Brooklyn, Ithaca, Wilmington, Kitchener, Canada, and from many other areas.

Many visitors came alone and then returned again and again with small groups of friends. Others came in large, organized groups.

Thirty-one Garden Clubs visited the garden, four groups came from the Public Housing Projects. The staff members of the City Planning Commission and staff members from the Department of Licenses and Inspections made a tour of the garden.

Two groups came from the University of Pennsylvania, one from the School of Education, the other from the Human Resources Project which asked to bring sixty-five members of the Youth Job Corps to the garden for a special briefing on community work projects. An interesting exhibit was arranged for this group to accompany the talk.

Another interesting group was composed of Extension Agents from Pennsylvania State University and Rutgers University in New Jersey.

The Young Wives' Club from the Y.W.C.A. also came to visit the Garden. They brought their lunches and enjoyed them in the Garden House.

The city-wide 4-H Club Identification Contest was held in the Demonstration Garden. And in July the suburban Upper Dublin 4-H Club held one of its stated meetings in the Demonstration Garden. Representatives from all our local 4-H Clubs were present with their Adult Leaders and in many cases with their parents. The evening held much of interest and inspiration for all who were present.

On July 5th an article by Hannah Lees about the Demonstration Garden was published in the Magazine Section of the Sunday Bulletin, under the title:

"Don't Have a Yard! Have a Garden!"

The response was immediate and tremendous! On that Sunday afternoon more than 150 people from every section of the city and from near and distant suburbs visited the Demonstration Garden.

During the spring of 1965 the area on the upper level of the Demonstration Garden was completely redesigned to provide a gracious entrance to the Mary Evans Memorial House. The Garden Club of Philadelphia sponsored the foundation planting and the Society of Little Gardens planted the lovely border on the west side of the terrace.

On the left as one approaches the house there is a beautiful little garden which has come to be known at The Sanctuary Garden, the name having been suggested by one of our local leaders. A tall planting of evergreens forms the background for the charming small statue, a gift of the sculptress, Margaret Wasserman Levy. Below the wall upon which the statue stands there is a small pool, with a grass panel in the foreground.

Many interesting events took place in the Demonstration Garden during the summer of 1965. An all-day Workshop was held for 4-H Club Leaders which included lectures and demonstrations and a practice period of planting the various units of the 4-H project gardens. The program ended with a flower identification contest.

The State Convention of the Garden Club Federation of Pennsylvania which met in Philadelphia included a visit to the Demonstration Garden on their program.

During the spring and autumn hundreds of children visited the Garden with their teachers.

In the summer of 1966 the Mantua Garden Club held a sale of geraniums in the Demonstration Garden, on the Saturday before Mother's Day. The pots were decorated with tinfoil and a little bow and were very gay and attractive.

Early in the afternoon two buses from New York arrived, bringing a group of welfare workers and many teen-agers. It was a delight to see their enthusiasm over the garden and many interesting questions were asked. When, at last, they returned to the buses almost every boy and girl was proudly holding a beautiful geranium to take home for a Mother's Day gift. With the proceeds from the sale the Mantua Garden Club purchased a fine kitchen cabinet as a gift for the Mary Evans House.

The Demonstration Garden has become a vital and constructive force in stimulating interest in community improvement and many people who have visited it have gone away with the thought, "We have a vacant lot on our block and it could look like that!" or "That Garden in a Box is just what I need in my back yard!"

As someone once remarked, "It is like a Flower Show which isn't taken down at the end of the week."

THE NEIGHBORHOOD GARDEN ASSOCIATION
TENTH ANNIVERSARY
1953 TO 1963

RECORD OF ACCOMPLISHMENT

- 385 Garden Blocks
- 16 Community Gardens
- 12 Play Areas on Vacant Lots
- 1,200 Doorway Gardens in Public Housing Projects
- 297 Individual 4-H Club project Gardens
- The Demonstration Teaching Garden

At the time of the Annual Meeting of the Board of Directors in April a gala luncheon was held in the Rose Garden at the Bellevue to celebrate the Tenth Anniversary of the Association and to honor the many sponsoring Garden Clubs and other groups.

Special recognition was given to the Garden Clubs which had worked with the Association since its founding in 1953.

Mr. Edmund N. Bacon, Executive Director of the City Planning Commission, was the speaker on the occasion.

The program closed with a showing of the slides of some of the Garden Blocks and the vacant lot gardens.

The tenth Annual Award Dinner of The Neighborhood Garden Association was held on November 12th.

The highlight of the occasion was the award of a special citation to Elizabeth J. Forrester, our Executive Secretary, and the presentation of a gift, in recognition of her dedicated service to the Association.

Hungarian couple planting their box

A Garden Block
in a Lithuanian area

During the past ten years The Neighborhood Garden Association has worked with many Races and Nationalities.

English	Lithuanian
Hungarian	Moorish
Irish	Negro
Italian	Polish
Kalmuck	Puerto Rican

The Association has worked with thousands of people in the underprivileged areas of the city and has been able to establish friendship and understanding among many diverse groups. This has been eloquently expressed in a report by one of the members of the Oasis Garden Club.

Excerpt from an Area Report. . . .

The Neighborhood Garden Association has done a great deal in fostering the Good Neighbor policy. I wish to thank the members of the Association for teaching us how to be good neighbors and how to work together toward common goals of understanding in this changing world.

Louise West
President of the Oasis Garden Club
Western Community Area

THE 4-H CLUB PROGRAM

During 1963 seven new 4-H Clubs were organized, bringing the total number of clubs to 29, with a membership of 300 boys and girls.

Mrs. Forrester held three Workshops each month for the 4-H Adult Leaders —one in North Philadelphia, one in South Philadelphia and one in West Philadelphia. These workshops were of tremendous value to the men and women who have become our local 4-H Club Leaders. The Workshops included demonstrations of new 4-H Club projects, plans for future club meetings were discussed, and when problems arose help was offered.

With great skill and incredible zeal Mrs. Harcom, Chairman of the 4-H Club Committee, helped the members convert trash-filled lots into pleasant flower gardens.

Under the dynamic leadership of Mr. James C. Kemp, the Area 4-H Agent, much was accomplished during 1965.

Ten new Clubs were organized. Four members attended the 4-H Club Congress at Pennsylvania State University. One member attended the 4-H Club Citizenship Course in Washington and another member attended a Leadership Training Course.

Four Clubs received county certificates in the Community Beautification Contest, and the Oasis Green Thumb 4-H Club received first place in the state Competition.

At the Annual Dinner Mr. Kemp received a special citation in recognition of his dedicated service and his inspiring leadership.

THOUGHTS FROM PHILADELPHIA'S 4-H CLUB MEMBERS

On the last page of each 4-H Club Project Book members are asked to record their thoughts about 4-H. The following are selections from the Plan and Plant For Beauty Project Books.

"I liked the day we were going to plant our flowers. It finally came and the heavens felt like they were on earth and I enjoyed it."

Victoria Ann   (age 11)

"4-H is fun and I think whoever started 4-H started a loving thing, and I hope we keep up the good work."   Francine   (age 10)

"Well I like the color of the ageratum. And I like the 4-H Club very much, it helps better learning, better loyalty and it makes your Housing Project a better project."   Ingrid   (age 10)

"I think it is a good thing to be in the 4-H Club. I like all of the plants and now I can learn to do better things and learn the names of all the flowers. I enjoy being in the club. We have fun. And something else about the club

—the girls and boys are friendly and we learn to get along with each other and that is the most important thing in the club." Alma   (age 11)

"The 4-H Club means a lot to me. The 4-H stands for: Head to clearer thinking, Heart to greater loyalty, Hands to larger service, Health to better living. The 4-H Club gives many children as myself a better chance to learn, and a lot of children a job when they have nothing to do. This is what makes children steal and rob drunkards for lak of something to do. This has given me a chance to learn about food in case the tragedy should acure that my father was out of work and my mother could not get any food for the children I can go to work to pick on farms to get money to help my mother. And after I am too old to be in 4-H Club I can teach my children to be 4-Hers to teach others from robbery and stealing." Marlene   (age 12)

"I planted my garden on June 2, 1962. When I planted my garden I wanted to win a ribbon. I came and watered my garden, pulled the weeds and pinched the flowers. When they were grown I took some home. They were so beautiful I kept them in the dining room and first room."
                                                  Edward   (age 13)

"My garden seemed to interest me a lot. I like working in my garden. I found new flowers I didn't know existed. As I worked in my garden I found not only was it work, it was fun and I work in my garden with all my love from the bottom of my heart."   Brenda   (age 13)

"My second year in 4-H clubing hasn't been a picnic. The problems were numerous. Since I have told you that we had problems I think you should know some. The late start thanks to some neighboring kids. The fence that suddenly disappeared. But that is only the beginning. After we planted our flowers they pulled up the flowers and wrecked the garden. But we did not give up. We worked and worked until they gave up. And about time too! Since then we have come a long ways. We are involved in a difficult task of rearranging the lot. But we could not have done it without the help of the Garden Association because when the spirits were low they gave them a lift."   Stanley   (age 13)

The main thing I like in a 4-H life is the plants and the help of the leader. I really like to learn the names of the plants, and it makes me feel real good noing I am a 4-H girl."   Elizabeth   (age 14)

"My garden in 4-H has been very interesting to me. I like to know the plants and how to take care of them. If I can I would like to stay in 4-H until I become a leader and can show other people what the 4-H Club has taught me."   Eleanor   (age 14)

"Before joining the 4-H Club I was not as interested in flowers as I am now. You can learn a lot of interesting things about flowers which are essential as far as education is concerned. I enjoy 4-H and hope to remain a member of the most fabulous idea ever thought of and now which is scattered all over the country." Barbara (age 15)

"This year marks my second year as a member of the 4-H Club and I can sum what it means in four easy words:

Love Friendship Care Warm

Love stands for the love and affection you share as you watch your flowers grow and realize what you have done with your own hands.

Care stands for the labor you have done to enable them to grow. It also stands for the little, small things, such as pulling weeds which we think is unimportant and really is a big thing.

Warm is the spot in your heart which you have reserved for the pride and joy you have of raising your flowers. Finally we have *friendship*. The friendly rivalry that takes place between the clubs and the feeling you have of having a winning club. But most of all I have gathered wisdom and experience of learning how to raise and care for flowers. This is what 4-H means to me." Deborah (age 15)

"My garden has been a very enjoyable and interesting project for me. It gave me a sense of responsibility and also a great love of nature. I found my club interesting to work with. Everyone seemed so enthused and excited. Up until this year I never enjoyed flowers. The 4-H Club did a lot to change that and I am very glad." Kathleen (age 15)

A garden of her own

THE MARY EVANS HOUSE

Through the generosity of the family of Miss Mary Evans The Neighborhood Garden Association became the recipient of a gift to be used as a memorial to her.

Miss Evans was an ardent gardener throughout her life, and a very active Garden Club member. She wrote on many horticultural subjects for publication in garden magazines, and was always generous in sharing her knowledge and her experience with others.

Through a remarkable series of coincidences the building adjacent to the Demonstration Garden became vacant at this time and it was agreed by the donors and The Neighborhood Garden Association that this would be a most fitting memorial to Mary Evans whose life-long interests had been people and gardens, and the furtherance of the dignity of the less fortunate classes.

For many years The Neighborhood Garden Association had realized that there was great need for headquarters in the city, but there were no funds to meet this need. It seemed that at last the dream was to become a reality.

The house had been occupied by six families living in two-room apartments and it was in deplorable condition. The Department of Licenses and Inspections had given the owner three chances to bring the house up to Housing Code Standards, but these warnings had been ignored. Therefore the house had been declared unfit for habitation, and all the tenants had been moved out and relocated.

On the 26th day of February in 1965 the final settlement was made, conveying to the Neighborhood Garden Association the ownership of the house at 3723 Mt. Vernon Street in Philadelphia.

The first thing to be undertaken was to have plans made for complete renovation of the house, and to have them approved by the proper authorities.

It was no easy task to obtain the measurements of every partition, every doorway, every window. It was bitterly cold, as there was no heat in the house, and it was darker than night, as all the windows had been sealed up with tin to prevent entry or breakage, and not one ray of light penetrated the darkness.

This meant slow progress. In order to record the feet and inches someone had to hold the largest electric lantern available while the architect put the measurements on the plan.

At last the plans had been completed and approved by the Neighborhood Garden Association and by the city authorities. Specifications were then drawn up and sent out for bids.

Application had been made to two Foundations for grants to help meet the expenses which would be incurred in connection with the renovation of the house. Fortunately the amounts requested were granted, and by spring it was possible to begin work on the house. Some people call it The House of the Three Miracles—first the memorial, then the availability of the house, and the two grants.

The plans included a long-needed office, a large room where meetings and many other activities could be held, a charming little reception room opening onto the terrace which overlooks the Demonstration Garden, and a small kitchen where refreshments can be prepared.

The second floor is devoted entirely to activities for children. There is a well-equipped workshop for boys, and a craft room for girls, a small library for children of various ages, and a very small print shop for older boys.

The members of the House Committee, Mrs. Richard C. Bull, Chairman, worked with dedicated zeal to create an atmosphere of simple charm, and the rooms radiate a feeling of warmth and welcome. The pieces of furniture and the draperies were chosen with great care.

DEDICATION OF THE MARY EVANS HOUSE

On September 22nd, 1965, the Mary Evans House was dedicated as the headquarters of The Neighborhood Garden Association, being the fulfillment of a long-cherished dream.

It was a radiant autumn afternoon and the many friends who had gathered for the occasion watched the simple ceremony from the terrace and the garden. Mrs. John Randall cut the ribbon and after a few gracious remarks, an excerpt from a brief account of the life of Mary Evans which Mrs. Randall had written was read by Mrs. Bush-Brown.

"We feel that the Mary Evans House is about as perfect a memorial to Aunt Polly as one could find. To combine her love of gardening with her deep interest in humanity—to counter the injustices of the world that concerned her so deeply, to help people who had not had her opportunities to be among her beloved flowers and derive the God-given strength that comes from community with nature, is to perpetuate the real Aunt Polly. We all feel that she would have loved it!"

The Mary Evans House has made it possible for The Neighborhood Garden Association to widen its sphere of service tremendously.

Board Meetings, Committee meetings, meetings of local and suburban garden clubs are held there.

One of the greatest advantages of having headquarters in the city is that we now have a place where we can welcome visitors from a distance. To be able to hold conferences there and to show slides to small delegations and to be able to offer the hospitality of mid-morning coffee or luncheon are the greatest satisfactions. Flower Shows and Christmas Workshops are held there, as well as many other activities.

LECTURES

During 1965 thirty lectures were given to garden clubs, church groups, the Ohio Federation of Garden Clubs, the Mid-Western Conference of Garden Clubs and the Conference of the Province of Washington Episcopal Church.

Seven television appearances were made by Mrs. Forrester.

In early April Mrs. Bush-Brown was asked to give two lectures in Washington: one to the National Capital Garden Club League, the other to a group of Settlement House Workers and Public Housing administrators.

Later in the month she was invited by Mrs. Lyndon B. Johnson to be the guest of honor at a White House Luncheon, where she spoke on Garden Blocks for American Cities.

In May she was asked to serve as a member of the Citizens Action Panel at the White House Conference on Natural Beauty, with an attendance of more than 800 participants and delegates. In reporting on the conference the publisher of a large magazine stated: "One of the highlights of the conference was the wonderful slide presentation of the Philadelphia Project."

YOUTH PROGRAM

The Youth Program initiated by The Neighborhood Garden Association is a unique, profit-sharing program which has proved to be very rewarding to the boys and girls who have participated. It offers not only an opportunity to acquire valuable skills and to earn some money; it develops a sense of pride and satisfaction which comes as a result of worthy accomplishment. The program meets some of the greatest needs of children growing up in the blighted areas of the city, and there are few such opportunities.

BOYS' PROGRAM

There is a ready sale for the articles which are made in the workshop. In order to make the project realistic the cost of the material used is deducted from the sale price. The young craftsman who made the article receives the balance.

The Association has been fortunate in having an exceptionally well qualified instructor for this program. Mr. Robinson is a faculty member in one of our public high schools in Philadelphia. He has fine leadership with the boys and is skilled in all phases of shop work.

During the summer classes are scheduled for morning and afternoon from Monday through Thursday. Fridays are devoted to field trips. During the school year classes are scheduled for Saturday mornings and afternoons. Boys participating in the program range from 8 to 15 years of age.

There is a great demand for the sturdy, well-built window boxes which the boys make. Good quality lumber which is treated with a non-toxic wood preservative is used. The boxes are reinforced with steel tape and will give many years of service. Larger plant boxes are made for special orders. Hanging plant baskets, bird houses and bird feeders are also popular items.

GIRLS' PROGRAM

Under the skilled and creative leadership of our Secretary, Mrs. Lawrence Jones, the girls' program has been an outstanding success. The girls have made many very attractive dish gardens. The table mats and dainty correspondence and greeting cards, pressed flowers being used for the motif, have been popular items and many repeat orders have come in for them.

The classes for the girls are scheduled for two afternoons a week throughout the year, except for holiday periods. Many articles were made for the delightful Christmas Bazaar which the girls held early in December.

FIELD TRIPS

Realizing that Field Trips are vital experiences in learning, it was decided to plan a series of trips on Fridays during the summer months for those participating in the Work Shop Program.

It is difficult for those who are not familiar with conditions in the congested, impoverished areas of the city to realize how restricted the horizons are for the children who are growing up there. Many of them have never seen a dawn or a sunset. They have never heard the song of a bird or seen a butterfly. And many of them have never seen grass or a flower.

The trips were varied and interesting, and the response was enthusiastic. There was a trip to the Schuylkill Valley Nature Center which was a thrilling experience for everyone. There was a walking tour through the historic area of Philadelphia where they saw the Liberty Bell and many other interesting things. There was a seven-mile hike along the Wissahickon, a visit to the Zoo, and an exciting ride on the Show Boat on the Delaware River.

LEADERSHIP TRAINING

Early in the spring of 1967 Mrs. Forrester organized a series of ten Leadership Training Workshops, known as *Operation Know How*. The Workshops were held one evening a week in the Mary Evans House.

The program was a very creative one and was of tremendous benefit to all who attended.

At the close of the series graduation exercises were held and certificates were awarded to those who completed the course.

NEIGHBORHOOD GARDEN CLUBS

There are four Neighborhood Garden Clubs, each serving a very large area within the city:

Berean Center Garden Club in North Philadelphia
Mantua Garden Club in West Philadelphia
Oasis Garden Club in Center City
The Oliver Jones Garden Club in South Philadelphia

These Neighborhood Garden Clubs carry on many interesting activities and maintain close contacts with their parent organization, The Neighborhood Garden Association of Philadelphia.

The Berean Garden Club has organized a Senior Citizens group and has brought cheer and beauty into the lives of the many lonely older people in their community. Each year the Club gives a Christmas dinner for the Senior Citizens group, and during the summer picnics and special trips are planned. The Senior Citizens meet twice a month to work on craft and garden projects.

The Mantua Garden Club has a series of Plant Sales each year during the spring. This is very helpful as it provides a place where people on Garden Blocks which have become Independent Blocks after two years of sponsorship can purchase their flowers. A special sale of geraniums is always held on the Saturday before Mothers' Day. The Mantua Garden Club has presented a number of beautiful gifts to the Mary Evans House out of the proceeds from these sales.

EXHIBIT IN
THE PHILADELPHIA FLOWER SHOW, 1966

For the first time in many years the Neighborhood Garden Association had an exhibit in the 1966 Philadelphia Flower Show.

Under the able co-chairmanship of Mrs. John K. Wilcox and Mrs. Charles S. Truitt, assisted by Mrs. Edward T. Stuart, Mr. and Mrs. Richard H. Hooper and Mr. and Mrs. George Wharton Pepper, III, the exhibit was an outstanding success.

The front of a small brick house was erected and with its window boxes was typical of the houses on many of our Garden Blocks. An attractively designed bulletin board on an easel gave many interesting facts about The Neighborhood Garden Association.

Throughout the day and evening slides depicting the many facets of our work were shown on an automatic projector.

The exhibit brought our Garden Block program to the attention of thousands of people attending the Flower Show.

GERANIUM PROJECT

In the spring of 1966 The Neighborhood Garden Association initiated a Geranium Project which proved to be of great interest to everyone who visited the Demonstration Garden.

The purpose was to determine which varieties of geraniums were heavy bloomers and which were light bloomers.

Twelve readily available varieties were selected and were planted three in a box. They were grown under identical conditions. The number of blooms produced by each box was carefully recorded and totaled at the end of the season with the following results:

Picardy 194;   Enchantress Fiat 167;   Irene 120;
Dawn 116;   Salmon Fiat 107;   Genie 106;
Salmon Irene 104;   Summer Cloud 77;   Charlotte 61

In the popularity poll the variety Enchantress Fiat received the greatest number of votes.

EXHIBIT IN
THE PHILADELPHIA FLOWER SHOW, 1967

Our very creative Co-Chairmen, Mrs. George Wharton Pepper III and Mrs. Alan McIlhenny, with the assistance of other members of the Board of Directors, staged an outstanding exhibit which received a Pennsylvania Horticultural Society Award of Merit.

A model of the Garden House in the Demonstration Garden was constructed on a much smaller scale by Mr. Robinson with the help of some of the boys in the Youth Program.

The exhibit was unique and charming with its lovely hanging baskets and flower boxes, and it attracted a great deal of attention. Almost everyone who passed along the aisle stopped for a few moments to look at the color photographs showing the various phases of our work, which were attractively displayed in the alcoves.

Mrs. John K. Willcox made a superb arrangement of vegetables in a beautiful copper container which was considered one of the most outstanding arrangements in the entire show.

During the winter the Co-Chairmen of the exhibit had prepared a very attractive small folder to be given out at the time of the Flower Show. Under the direction of Mr. Bush-Brown, they set the type and printed several hundred copies in the Print Shop at the Mary Evans House. These supplied the answers to some of the questions which were asked during the Flower Show.

Members of the Board of Directors served as hostesses at the exhibit.

MRS. LYNDON B. JOHNSON'S VISIT

The visit of Mrs. Johnson to the Demonstration Garden on the 10th of June, 1966, was a memorable event which will be cherished in the hearts of countless people.

Mrs. Johnson's route included passing through some of the Garden Blocks where hundreds of people had gathered on the sidewalks to wave a welcome to her.

Fortunately the flash thunderstorm which heralded her approach to the

Demonstration Garden was soon over and later the garden was flooded with sunshine.

Upon her arrival Mrs. Johnson presented to The Neighborhood Garden Association a beautiful young magnolia tree grown from a cutting taken from a magnolia tree on the White House grounds which was planted by President Andrew Jackson.

A reception committee, including members of the Board of Directors and several of our Garden Block Leaders, greeted Mrs. Johnson in the Garden House and she was then taken on a tour of the Demonstration Garden by Mrs. Bush-Brown.

With her dedication to the ideal of a more beautiful America, Mrs. Johnson was interested in every aspect of our work and it was a joy to share with her some of our past accomplishments and our hopes for the future.

THE SYMPOSIUM

Each year an increasing number of letters are received by The Neighborhood Garden Association from people who have heard about our Garden Block Program and wish to initiate a similar project in their own community.

It had long been our hope that some day we would be able to plan for a Symposium which would enable people to see our program in action. In the spring of 1967 this long-cherished dream became a reality, made possible through the generosity of an anonymous donor.

An interesting two-day program was held on May 10th and 11th. After registering at the Warwick Hotel, where headquarters had been set up, the delegates visited the Demonstration Garden, and luncheon was served in the Mary Evans House.

In the afternoon there was a tour of the Garden Blocks, Vacant-lot Gardens and 4-H Club Gardens. There was also an opportunity to see the actual planting of a Garden Block.

A reception and festive dinner was held at the Warwick that evening, a member of the Board of Directors serving as hostess at each table. Following the dinner Dr. Sweeney spoke as a representative of the Board and Mrs. Forrester gave an account of what she considered a typical day in the life of the Executive Director. A Garden Block Leader gave the audience many interesting personal insights as she told how much the flower boxes meant to the residents on her block. Mrs. Bush-Brown spoke about the founding of The Neighborhood Garden Association in 1953, and touched briefly on some of the most significant accomplishments. The evening closed with a lively question and answer period.

On the following morning there were a series of Discussion Meetings and Workshops on Leadership Training, Youth Groups and Special Events.

After a farewell luncheon there was an optional tour of Independence Hall and the Society Hill area.

Forty-five delegates attended the Symposium, representing widely scattered areas: Baltimore, Md., Greenville, S.C., Pittsburgh, Penna., Plainfield, N.J., Providence, R.I., Sewickley, Penna., Summit, N.J., Washington, D.C. and many others areas.

Early in the summer delegates from Baltimore, Pittsburgh, and Providence reported that they had organized their Garden Block Programs. Other delegates later reported that they planned to initiate their Garden Block programs in the early spring of 1968.

YOUTH DEVELOPMENT CENTER

In early July, 1967, The Neighborhood Garden Association received a telephone call from the Administrator of the Youth Development Center at Fort Mifflin, asking if we could give them some help and advice. This is a Center for "hard core" boys between 16 and 19 years of age.

Upon our first visit we were taken on a tour of the grounds and at one point we saw in the distance a small tree with large pink blossoms. When we came to it we found to our amazement that the flowers had been made out of pink crepe paper and had been carefully wired onto the branches. Nearby was a small plot filled with crepe paper flowers in various colors. In those very grim surroundings the boys had been so hungry for a little touch of beauty that they had, on their own initiative, done this.

As an outcome of this first visit the boys, under the supervision of an instructor, made 32 window boxes, one for each window on the Administration Building and on the converted marine barracks which are used as dormitories. These were planted with beautiful, large red geraniums and white petunias, and what a lift they gave to the place!

Plans were made for long flower borders along the sides of the barracks where each boy would have his own plot, and a little park-like area near the Administration Building was designed as a sitting place for parents when they came on week-ends to visit their sons. The plan included a very small play area for small children when they came with the parents.

Teaching and learning

OPERATION OUT-REACH

ENGLAND

Several years ago Mr. Michael Dower, a town planner from England, had an opportunity to see the slides showing the work of The Neighborhood Garden Association. He was so impressed that he asked if he could have a duplicate set to take back when he returned to England. He has reported that these have been shown many times with the result that Garden Blocks have been organized in some of the industrial cities in England.

The following letter was received from a social worker in London:

"Several years ago I heard Mr. Dower speak about his experiences in Philadelphia and now I am delighted that the Churchill Memorial Trust has awarded me a fellowship to study the work at first hand. I am enormously excited by your work since, as a Borough Councillor in the London Borough of Islington, I am particularly concerned to involve our citizens in the improvement of their own neighborhoods."

BALTIMORE

A lecture on the Philadelphia Garden Block program was given in Baltimore in the spring of 1966. The response was so enthusiastic that a bus trip to Philadelphia was arranged for a date in June. In the group were members of the Baltimore Beautification Committee and members of the Urban Renewal Agency, as well as many Garden Club members. As a result of the visit a most successful Garden Block program was launched the following spring.

HARRISBURG

As a result of visiting our Philadelphia Garden Blocks the previous autumn, the Garden Club of Harrisburg planted its first Garden Block in May, 1966, and it was an exciting and rewarding experience for everyone involved.

A few days later the residents on the block formed a Garden Club and decided to hold a rummage sale to raise money to buy paint and garbage cans for the block. Within a few weeks a number of neighboring streets had become Garden Blocks.

In August a large meeting was held on a play lot adjacent to the first Garden Block. Residents from all the Garden Blocks and many city officials from the Mayor's office, the Department of Education and other city departments attended the meeting.

An excellent program was presented, including reports from the Block Leaders, and the showing of the slides of some of the Philadelphia Garden Blocks.

Before the evening was over The Neighborhood Garden Association of Harrisburg had been officially organized.

NEW YORK CITY

In the autumn of 1964 the Executive Director of the Park Association of New York, a private organization, visited Philadelphia and was taken on a tour of the Garden Blocks. His visit was followed by a visit from two members of the Board of Trustees of the Association.

In the spring of 1965 a pilot Garden Block was organized by Mrs. Donald Johnson, a member of the Board of Trustees, in the Bedford-Stuyvesant area of Brooklyn. The response was so enthusiastic that the project soon became a five-block project. In 1966 five new blocks were organized in the area and a Community Garden was developed.

In addition, five block projects were initiated in the Saint Nicholas Park area in central Harlem, and two projects in the Metro-North section of East Harlem.

At the close of the season Mrs. Donald Johnson, the Chairman, wrote, "We are increasingly convinced that the block association is a most effective unit through which to achieve neighborhood improvement and beautification. Your association has been of immeasurable help to us in beginning our program in New York."

PITTSBURGH

In September 1966 a delegation from Pittsburgh was taken on a tour of our Garden Blocks and the Demonstration Garden. As a result of this visit an illustrated lecture on the work of the Neighborhood Garden Association was given to a group of Garden Club members in Pittsburgh and a Garden Block program was launched in the spring of 1967.

Later in the season a letter from a man connected with the program closed with the sentence: "It has done just what you said it would do!"

THE CHRISTMAS WORKSHOPS

In November 1967 three Christmas Workshops were held in the Mary Evans House to instruct leaders how to organize similar workshops in their own communities. The 58 persons who attended the Workshop represented Garden Blocks in every section of the city.

Many attractive and creative arrangements were brought in for display by members of some of the sponsoring groups.

Supplies such as wreath frames, tinsel, ribbons, and other items were on hand for sale at cost, to those attending the Workshop.

As a result of these Workshops held by Mrs. Forrester in the Mary Evans House, 23 Christmas Workshops were held in various parts of the city.

The Neighborhood Garden Association had a ton of Christmas greens shipped down from Canada, and the Garden House in the Demonstration Garden became an outdoor Christmas Workshop. The greens were sorted and tied in small bundles and sold at cost to the various groups on the Garden Blocks. At Christmas time hundreds of members had beautiful wreaths or swags on their doors.

RECOGNITION

Over the years The Neighborhood Garden Association has received the following Awards and Citations:

1960 *PUBLIC HOUSING AUTHORITY*
A Citation to
The Neighborhood Garden Association
of Philadelphia
for
Distinguished Service and
Dedicated Leadership
in making
Richard Allen Homes
a Better Place to Live

1961 *NATIONAL COUNCIL OF STATE GARDEN CLUBS*
a Citation
in recognition of the distinguished service
of The Neighborhood Garden Association
in Depressed Areas.

1962 *PENNSYLVANIA HORTICULTURAL SOCIETY*
Award of Merit to
The Neighborhood Garden Association
of Philadelphia
for providing tangible proof of what can

be accomplished through gardening to
restore neighborhood pride and renew
human dignity, in a program which has
been emulated by many other
communities.

1963 *THE COUNCIL OF THE CITY OF PHILADELPHIA*

Whereas, Delegations have come from Baltimore, Boston, Buffalo, New York City, St. Louis and Wilmington to see and learn about Philadelphia's Garden Block Program, and requests for information concerning the Garden Block Program have come from many countries abroad; therefore

Resolved, By the Council of the City of Philadelphia, That we hereby commend The Neighborhood Garden Association of Philadelphia for ten years of accomplishment in encouraging and fostering an interest in flowers and gardening in the congested areas of the City.

Resolved, That an engrossed copy of this Resolution be presented to the President of The Neighborhood Garden Association of Philadelphia, Mrs. James Bush-Brown, as evidence of the sincere sentiments of this legislative body. The twenty-sixth day of September, 1963.

Paul D'Ortona
President of City Council

1964 *A NATIONAL HONOR*

The George Washington Honor Medal
for the 1964 Civic Pride Project
was awarded to The Neighborhood Garden Association of Philadelphia,
by the Trustees and Officers of the Freedoms Foundation at Valley Forge

Nominations for this Award are received from every section of the country, and it is a significant honor to be selected as a recipient.

Mrs. Charles S. Truitt prepared the attractive brochure portraying the work of The Neighborhood Association which was sent to the Award Committee after word had been received that our Association had been nominated.

1966 *PENNSYLVANIA HORTICULTURAL SOCIETY*

A Gold Medal Certificate
Presented jointly to The Neighborhood Garden Association and the Philadelphia Extension Service. The Garden is a fine demonstration of what can be done in the city. It is a jewel in the midst of a blighted area and it has served as an inspiration to thousands.

REMARKS TO REMEMBER

"I've lived on this block for 48 years but I've never seen a flower on it before." remarked an old lady of 83 as she finished planting her window box and stood looking at it with loving pride.

The first flowers
ever on her block

"When I'm working with the soil it makes me feel real humble. I think with me it's sort of a form of prayer." said a man as he stood looking at the flower borders in the Demonstration Garden.

"Before it was just a house. Now it looks like a home." said a young woman with pride and joy.

"Every morning before I go into the kitchen to get breakfast I always come out on the porch and stand here for a few minutes just to look at my garden. It makes my day." remarked a housewife who had a little dooryard garden filled with bloom.

"When I came in here this morning I felt so depressed that life didn't seem worth living." said a young woman as she was about to leave the Demonstration Garden. "Now I know it is worth while!" She had walked about the garden and then had sat quietly in the Garden House for nearly an hour and had been able to resolve some of her problems.

The old man who was planting his window box handled each plant with gentle care. I watched him for a few minutes and then remarked, "I guess you grew up in the country." "No," he replied, "I was born and raised here in the city. I've never been to the country." All that he had ever known during his seventy years were the bleak, treeless areas of South Philadelphia. As he finished planting his flower box he turned to me with a smile. "But I have a little bit of country at my window now." he said.

And for many others their window boxes on the Garden Blocks may be the only bit of country they will ever know.

A LETTER TO BE CHERISHED

Dear Members of the Neighborhood Garden Association, It has been a pleasure to know and work with people like you. Our lives have been enriched and blessed.

I am sure that we will cherish sweet recollections of our work and friendship together.

May God bless and keep you all in your great work of beautifying our city and lifting the hearts and minds of people.

Rev. and Mrs. General Lee Griffin
Garden Block Leaders

EXPANDING HORIZONS

In the year 1653 William Bradford, Governor of the Plymouth Colony, wrote "Thus out of small beginnings greater things have been produced . . . and as one small candle may light a thousand, so the light here kindled hath shone unto many."

On that May morning in 1953 when our first Garden Block was planted on 700 Mercy Street in South Philadelphia, little did any of us realize that a candle had been lighted which would become a beacon to so many.

The Garden Block programs has proved to be such a successful counter-attack against the spread of urban blight that it has received national and international recognition.

Each year hundreds of requests for information concerning the program of The Neighborhood Garden Association are received. Delegations have come from many areas to learn about Philadelphia's Garden Block program, and similar programs have been initiated in many other cities, among them:

Baltimore, Md.	Columbus, Ohio	Providence, R. I.
Boston, Mass.	Harrisburg, Penna.	Summit, N. J.
Brooklyn, N. Y.	New York City	Trenton, N. J.
Chicago, Ill.	Pittsburgh, Penna.	Washington, D. C.
Cincinnati, Ohio	Plainfield, N. J.	Wilmington, Del.

Requests for information have also been received from several foreign countries,—Australia, England, Greece, Holland, India, and Japan.

ACCOMPLISHMENTS

The work of The Neighborhood Garden Association has had a tremendous impact upon the lives and the environment of more than 200,000 people in the congested areas of Philadelphia.

Each year since its founding the Association has been able to record figures which have shown steady growth. In 1953 there were 7 Garden Blocks. In 1968 there are well over 500 Garden Blocks. Heartening as this is, there are other things which cannot be presented in figures but are even more important. These are the intangibles, the things of the spirit, which have made the work of the Association so rewarding and its influence so far-reaching.

In depressed areas where the people were completely apathetic to their surroundings, The Neighborhood Garden Association has been able to instill new spirit and morale.

It has taught neighbors to work cooperatively together to improve their communities.

It has developed fine leaders in areas where there had been little or no opportunity for constructive leadership.

It has helped people to grow into an awareness of their responsibilities as concerned citizens.

It has fostered friendship and understanding between people of diverse nationalities and races.

Through the organization of 4-H Clubs and other Youth Projects it has created opportunities for boys and girls to use their energies constructively instead of destructively.

THE MOTTO

At the time of its founding it was agreed that the motto of The Neighborhood Garden Association would be:

"Strive to make the world a little better and more
beautiful because you have lived in it."

Edward Bok

As the years have passed thousands of people, young and old, have taken this motto into their hearts and have transformed hundreds of dreary streets into places of beauty, dignity, and pride. There are flower boxes at the windows, rose bays gay with bloom, and trash-filled vacant lots have become community gardens.

Each year has brought new opportunities for service to The Neighborhood Garden Association, and its areas of endeavor and its influences have been constantly extended.

Over the years the Association has proved the wisdom of the ancient Chinese proverb—

"It is better to light a candle
Than to curse the darkness."

A Garden Block in North Philadelphia

"I am constantly impressed with how infinitesimal is anything that I can do; yet I am even more impressed with how important it is that I do it." —*Herbert Spencer*

LIST OF ILLUSTRATIONS